luscious lemon desserts

luscious lemon desserts

by lori longbotham

photographs by alison miksch

CHRONICLE BOOKS
SAN FRANCISCO

ACKNOWLEDGMENTS

All my thanks go to my favorites—Deborah Mintcheff, Judith Sutton, Barbara Ottenhoff, Carlotta Kramer, Marie Regusis, Lisa Troland, Barbara Nell Howe, Susan Westmoreland, Rosey and Sprocket, Jean Pellegrino, Sabra Turnbull, Laura and Jessica, Dr. Bob, Auntie Jean, Mom and Ken, Steve and Liz, and Dad.

Gratitude also to the charming Bill LeBlond and the lovely Amy Treadwell for making it so easy and fun. I'm grateful to Benjamin Shaykin, Alison Miksch, Sara Neumeier, and Barbara Fritz, for such a splendid-looking book. I'm also much obliged to Angela Miller and Joan Ward.

Thank you, Jerry, for your endless kindness.

Library of Congress Cataloging-in-Publication Data:

Longbotham, Lori.
       Luscious lemon desserts / by Lori Longbotham.
            p. com.
       ISBN 0-8118-2893-X
       1. Desserts. 2. Cookery (Lemons) I. Title.

       TX773 .L586 2001
       641.8'6—dc21
                                    00-060354

Manufactured in China

The photographer wishes to dedicate her work to her father, who instilled in her a lifelong love of pictures.

Prop styling by Barbara Fritz
Food styling by Sara Neumeier
Designed by Benjamin Shaykin
Typeset in Vendetta, TheSans, Belizio, and Clarendon

Distributed in Canada by Raincoast Books
9050 Shaughnessy Street
Vancouver, British Columbia V6P 6E5

10 9 8 7

Chronicle Books LLC
85 Second Street
San Francisco, California 94105

www.chroniclebooks.com

contents

This book uses approximately 176 lemons.

introduction

LEMON SWEETS ARE THE DIVAS OF DESSERTS. They sing and dance on the palate, and it's not always a soft-shoe: They dance confidently, assertively, and even flamboyantly—like Rogers and Astaire on the wings of a biplane flying down to Rio.

Even a photo of plump, juicy lemons artfully arranged in a cobalt blue porcelain bowl tantalizes my appetite with visions of all the possibilities: lemon bars, lemon ice cream, lemon shortbread, lemon *panna cotta*, chilled lemon soufflé, and lemon cheesecakes. Lemon sweets range from the simple to the sublime, from the quick and easy to the most elaborate showstoppers, from the starkly minimal to curlicue baroque. They can be as homey your mother's lemon meringue pie (or lemon "lerangue," as we called it at my house); as featherlight as the crisp lemon wafers you munched on after school with a glass of cold milk; or as sophisticated as the sleek lemon tart you tasted on your first visit to Paris.

And now all your favorite lemon dessert recipes, along with some new and exciting ones (including some delightful surprises), can be found right here. *Luscious Lemon Desserts*, the first ever lemon dessert book, includes over seventy clearly written and thoroughly tested recipes, tons of serving suggestions, plus information on buying, storing, and using the fruit, and a handy guide to equipment and techniques.

Nothing says "sunshine" in the kitchen or on a menu like lemon. The lemon is a symbol of tart refreshment; its color and fragrance lift our spirits before we even taste it. We can enjoy lemon desserts all year-round, not just during a single season. Cooling in the summer, lemon desserts are perfect after a light alfresco repast under a beautiful shade tree. How about Lemon Meringue Ice-Cream Cake (page 29)? The warm comfort of a baked lemon dessert, such as Lemon Mascarpone-Clementine Gratins (page 74), is the perfect ending to a hearty winter feast in front of a cozy fire.

Lemons, like salt, bring out the flavors of other ingredients and make everything taste fresher and brighter. They work wonders in savory dishes, but they truly shine in desserts. Just a squeeze of juice, a paper-thin slice, or a curl of zest adds a piquant zing, a tart edge, and a lovely aroma. Lemon tastes good with almost everything. It marries with all sorts of herbs and spices, berries and other fruits, spirits and liqueurs, and even edible flowers.

I love sweet, but I love the combinations of bittersweet, sweet, and tart, and of sweet and

sour even more. Lemons are born that way, to contrast and balance. Maybe that's the secret to the "swooniness" of lemon desserts; lemons both balance and enhance all flavors.

One of the best things about lemon desserts is how readily they take to variations. Bake some fabulous crisp lemon wafers. Nothing could be better with a bowl of sorbet and berries. But add a fresh herb like thyme or rosemary to that cookie dough, and you'll have a fabulously sophisticated grown-up taste treat. Or make lemon sorbet. You can keep it pure and simple, but why not try flavoring it with a fresh herb: basil, tarragon, or lemon verbena would all be fabulous, or how about lemongrass? Herbs add a rich and complex effect, a finesse, and a fresh green flavor that strengthen and complement the flavor of lemon; but they are certainly not the cook's only option. Spices add a specific quality and dimension to a lemon dessert and may be just what a dish needs to lure the sweetness from other ingredients. Wines, liqueurs, and spirits are other quick and easy ways to add intense, interesting flavors to lemon desserts.

Every element of a lemon can be used in desserts—the zest, pulp, and juice. The essential oils in the zest add a subtle, yet lively layering of flavors. A squeeze of juice can provide the necessary acid note to perfectly balance the flavors of a dessert, and the lemon juice and zest lift and reveal flavors, mingle with and heighten flavors,

and can enhance and reveal flavors by balancing sweetness and richness.

Think of lemonade and how much better it is than plain sugar and water. That's exactly what lemon can do for a dessert. Close your eyes and put yourself in a chair in a lovely outdoor cafe in Paris. You're terribly thirsty after all that shopping. What should you order? Definitely the *citron pressé*, the perfect thirst quencher. It's just lemon juice and ice in a tall glass, served with a carafe of water, a small pitcher of sugar syrup, and a long spoon for a delicious and refreshing drink. As with a cold, frosty serving of all-American lemonade, the lemon adds a good dose of sour, but one that is well masked with sweet. The acid adds clean, dry, and refreshing tones.

So, turn that notorious old sourpuss, the lemon, into the sweetest thing you've ever tasted.

lemon aid LEMON DESSERT BASICS

Lemons are fresh, colorful, and fragrant all year-round; they know no season. They are the most versatile citrus, and the one that keeps the longest.

all about lemons

TYPES OF LEMONS There are three types of lemon: common, rough, and sweet. The tart yellow ones that most of us choose from the produce section of the local supermarket are common lemons: egg-shaped Eurekas in the summer and Lisbons in the fall. Rough lemons are used only as rootstock for other citrus. Sweet lemons are not really sweet, just less acidic. Meyer lemons—the small, round, thin-skinned variety favored by gourmets—are considered sweet lemons, although really they're just not sour. Look for them in specialty markets and on backyard trees, mostly in California.

HOW TO BUY LEMONS I grew up in California with lemon trees in the backyard, and we picked lemons whenever we wanted them. I will never forget the fragrance of those lemons and their blossoms. Now that I live in New York City, where the climate is not conducive to lemon trees (and most of us don't have backyards), I do my lemon shopping at local produce markets and in supermarkets. I am happy with the lemons I buy; their superb self-packaging allows them to be shipped, handled, and stored for long periods of time and still remain very high quality.

Supermarkets offer a year-round, reasonably priced supply of lemons. They're always there, glowing in the produce section, piled high and bright yellow. Unlike other varieties of citrus fruit, no distinction is made by retailers between the types of lemons available, largely because most of them have similar qualities. Some lemons have very fine skin and are slightly smaller and more rounded in shape. They usually have a thinner layer of pith under the rind and are therefore more attractive when cut for garnishes or decorations. The rougher, larger, and more elongated fruit tends to have a thicker layer of pith and often more seeds.

Always choose the freshest lemons. They should have lustrous, oily skins and be smooth and firm to the touch. Avoid blemished, bruised, and dry, wrinkled specimens. The thinner-skinned lemons usually contain more juice, and those with thicker skin tend to have more flavorful zest.

For juice, look for a lemon that is heavy in the hand, one that feels heavy with juice. The really rock hard lemons invariably yield little juice, so choose soft, ripe lemons. Citrus fruits from warmer climates may have a slightly green tinge to their skin; this does not mean they are not ripe.

HOW TO STORE LEMONS After you've picked out perfect lemons at the store, you need to treat them right when you bring them home; it does make a difference. If you are using the lemons within a few days, store them in a cool room in a basket—they yield more juice when they are stored at room temperature. If you are storing them longer, keep them in the refrigerator. They'll be good for up to 4 weeks in the fridge, and for about a week to 10 days at room temperature. Once cut, lemons last only about 2 days covered and refrigerated. After they've been zested, keep those bald lemons in a vegetable crisper in your refrigerator, and plan on juicing them within 1 week.

working with lemons

HOW TO SQUEEZE LEMONS If morning sunshine had a flavor, it would be lemon juice. Lemon's tart juice is the perfect complement to sugar; its lively and refreshing taste and high acid content give a perfect piquancy to desserts. You'll get the most juice from a lemon if you roll it on a counter beneath the palm of your hand or drop it in hot water for a few min-

utes before juicing. Then use one of the tools described on page 16. Don't discard the squeezed-out fruit. Toss it into poaching liquid when you're cooking fruit, or even rub it over copper pans with coarse salt to polish them.

One large lemon yields ¼ cup of juice; you'll get 1 cup of juice from 4 large lemons. If you'd like, store the juice, tightly covered, in the refrigerator for 1 week, or freeze the fresh juice in ice cube trays, using about 2 tablespoons per cube. After freezing them, store the cubes in a resealable plastic bag in the freezer.

USING THE ZEST Lemon juice plays an important role in dessert making, but it is the zest that adds the more complex and interesting flavor. The volatile aromatic oils contain floral notes and tangy tones as well as a sophisticated, pleasant bitterness. Zest underscores the lemon flavor of the juice and insinuates its sunny personality, adding zing, and brightening the flavor of desserts. Scratch the lemon in your hand— the more fragrant it is, the more flavorful the zest will be.

For me, most of the joy in a lemon is in the zest, where the aromatic flavor is. The essential oils in the zest give tremendous, lemony flavor and fragrance to desserts.

The first thing to do before zesting a lemon is to wash it thoroughly. Fortunately, most of the insecticides used on commercially grown citrus fruits are washed off after harvest. Then the fruit is disinfected and coated with a water-soluble wax for protection during shipping. So lemons need to be washed thoroughly, even scrubbed with soap and warm water, to remove the wax. If you want to avoid pesticides completely, use organic lemons, but even those should be washed thoroughly before using, as they are also often coated with wax.

There are many forms the zest can take: quarters of the lemon for candying, long wide strips for syrups and poaching, julienned zest for garnishing, and finely grated zest for flavoring desserts.

Grating the lemon zest is my favorite way to use it because it gives optimum flavor. It's that search for flavor power (as well as ease of preparation) that led me to the Microplane grater, and I'm totally convinced of its superiority. See pages 16 and 17 for descriptions of this tool and others for grating or removing the zest.

The zest of a lemon need never be wasted. Put it in a jar with granulated sugar if you can't use it immediately. A large lemon yields about 1 tablespoon of zest. The accurate measurement of the zest is crucial to the final balance of taste between sweet and sour, and using too much zest can cause bitterness. The lemon's volatile oils are strongest just after zesting, so remove the zest just before using. It's much easier to zest a whole lemon than one that has been cut, so zest before you juice.

SLICING LEMONS When you need decorative slices, cut them crosswise with your sharpest knife from the center of the lemon, and use the ends for squeezing.

COOKING LEMONS When cooking lemons, it is preferable to use nonreactive utensils, pots, and pans. Avoid cast iron and aluminum; lemon juice can react with these metals, causing unwanted flavor and color changes. If you are using only a small amount of juice or zest, a nonreactive pot is not as critical.

more tips, techniques, and tricks of the trade

BEATING EGG WHITES Always use a clean bowl and beaters. If I'm not absolutely confident that no vestige of egg yolk or other fat is lurking, I give the beaters and bowl a quick wash with a bit of vinegar and water. It also helps to use egg whites that are room temperature. It's easier to separate them when they're cold, but they foam better when they're room temperature. I've found it works best to beat the egg whites at medium speed until they foam, which should take 1 or 2 minutes. Then increase the speed to medium-high, add the salt, cream of tartar, or sugar (the stabilizing ingredients), and beat just to soft or stiff peaks, as the recipe requires. For soft peaks, beat the egg whites just enough so that when the mixer is turned off and the beaters are lifted, the foam makes peaks that fall over immediately. For stiff peaks, beat until the peaks stand straight up and stay there when the beaters are lifted.

COOKING TIMES When a range of times is given for doneness (for example, "Bake for 30 to 40 minutes"), always check after the first amount of time has elapsed and then watch closely.

FOLDING Folding is done to combine fragile ingredients (such as whipped egg whites) with a heavier mixture in a way that won't remove any of the air that's been beaten into the fragile ingredients. Use either a whisk or a rubber spatula and first add a small amount of the mixture you're folding in. Then turn the two mixtures together, cutting straight down through the center of the bowl; turn the whisk or spatula toward you, and lift up. Turn the bowl an inch or two and repeat. Continue this procedure, working around the bowl, just until no streaks remain. Then add more of the ingredients you're folding in and repeat the process.

MEASURING FLOUR How you measure the flour for a dessert recipe is crucial to the final outcome. When I measured the flour for these recipes, I stirred the flour in the canister, spooned it into the measuring cup, and leveled the top with a table knife. Dipping the measuring cup into the flour gives you a different amount of flour, so don't measure it that way for

these recipes. Another caveat: In the list of ingredients "1 cup flour, sifted" means measure the flour first and then sift. "1 cup sifted flour" means sift the flour first and then measure. Pay close attention. Whether you sift before or after measuring changes the quantity of the flour.

PREPARING CAKE PANS AND BAKING SHEETS Just smear the bottom and sides with softened butter. If the pan also needs to be floured, add the flour to the pan, then shake and turn it so that the sides and bottom are covered with a thin coating of flour. Turn the pan upside down over the sink and gently shake out any excess flour.

ROLLING OUT AND LIFTING PASTRY Press the dough flat on a smooth, lightly floured work surface. Sprinkle the dough and the rolling pin with flour, and roll out the dough in short, even strokes, working from the center out to the edge. Carefully fold the pastry over the rolling pin, lift gently, and drape it over the pan.

USING A PASTRY BAG Begin by inserting the tip you want to use, forcing it through the hole at the small end of the bag for a snug fit. Place the bag, tip end down, in a large glass measuring cup and fold the sides down around the outside of the cup. The tip end should rest curled against the bag to keep what's inside from oozing out while you're filling the bag. Using a rubber spatula, scoop the filling into the bag. Remove the bag from the cup and twist the opening so that it's closed. Hold the bag firmly with one hand just above the filling and use the other hand to guide the tip. Gently squeeze the filling out with the upper hand.

lemon garnishes

COG-WHEEL EDGES Use a channel knife to remove narrow, deep strips of the lemon rind along the length of the fruit before slicing crosswise.

CUTOUTS Pare the zest from the fruit in large pieces and cook it in boiling water for 10 minutes, then drain well. Use a small, sharp-pointed knife to cut diamonds or leaf shapes. Tiny aspic cutters may be used to stamp out flowers and other shapes.

ROSES Use a small, very sharp knife to cut the zest off the fruit in a long, thin strip, which will curl around slightly; do not cut any pith with the rind. Roll the lemon rind into a rose shape.

SHELLS Cut the top off a lemon and scoop out the fruit with a grapefruit spoon. Trim the bottom of the shell so that it stands steadily. Fill with sorbet or ice cream and freeze.

SLICES Large lemons with a thick layer of pith do not produce attractive slices, so look for small, slightly rounded fruit with comparatively fine-textured skin.

TWISTS Cut a fairly thin slice of fruit crosswise, then slit to the center of the fruit. Twist the cut edges of the slit in opposite directions so the slice can stand.

VANDYKE CUT Use a sharp pointed knife to cut around the middle of a lemon, cutting in as far as the center of the fruit and alternating the angle of each cut to create a zigzag pattern. When you have cut all around the fruit, pull the two halves apart.

WEDGES Used when the juice is to be squeezed over food before it is eaten.

ZEST STRIPS Pare the zest in long pieces and then cut into very fine strips. Use as is or blanch in boiling water for 10 minutes, drain, and use as a garnish.

ingredients

PURE LEMON EXTRACT Lemon extract is not my favorite way to get honest lemon flavor. It can be harsh and often tastes artificial. Fresh lemon juice and zest are so vastly superior that there's no reason to use it, except in a few desserts, when you need some extra help to really pack in that lemony taste. I use it only to punch up the flavor of a lemon dessert when I'm already adding fresh zest and/or juice.

PURE LEMON OIL You can substitute pure lemon oil for fresh lemon zest and/or juice. I love it; it's an easy way to add a fabulous, true lemon flavor. So, if you're twelve miles from a lemon and are craving the flavor, I highly recommend it. I always have lemon oil in my pantry, where it lasts indefinitely. The only brand I've ever seen is Boyajian, and it's available in specialty foods stores and through *The Baker's Catalogue* (800-827-6836). I tried using pure lemon extract in an angel food cake, which has no fat to round out the flavor, and it tasted quite a lot like lemon furniture polish. When I used pure lemon oil for the same cake, I liked it even more than fresh lemon, because the oil has no texture, unlike lemon zest. I've also been known to put pure lemon oil into my bath water.

LEMONCELLO Also spelled limonecello. However it's spelled, it's pronounced lee-mohn-CHEH-loh. A liqueur from Italy, more specifically the Amalfi Coast and Sicily, lemoncello is made by steeping lemon zest in alcohol and adding a sugar syrup. It has a wonderful, sunny, intense lemon flavor.

equipment

BLOWTORCH Available in a home kitchen size at many kitchenware shops and through Williams-Sonoma catalog (800-541-2233); it's in the mid-thirty-dollar range and is perfect for caramelizing the sugar on a crème brûlée. It gives you much more control than your broiler, no matter how great your broiler is. Its adjustable flame melts the sugar quickly, so the custard

doesn't overcook. A cook's blowtorch is compact (less than six inches long), has a comfortable rubber handle, and uses butane fuel.

ELECTRIC MIXERS I used a handheld mixer for each recipe in this book that requires a mixer. If you have a heavy-duty mixer, use it, especially when you're beating fourteen egg whites for the angel food cake; but you sure don't have to go out and buy one to use this book.

MEASURING CUPS Stainless steel cups are best for measuring dry ingredients. One-cup, 2-cup, 4-cup, and 8-cup glass measures are very handy to have in the kitchen for liquids.

MEASURING SPOONS Look for a heavy-duty metal set that won't bend easily and has four graduated spoons: 1 tablespoon, 1 teaspoon, ½ teaspoon, and ¼ teaspoon.

MIXING BOWLS Both the metal and glass versions are useful. Metal is great for using over hot water as the top of a double boiler. Glass is good for melting chocolate or butter in a microwave. It's impossible to have too many mixing bowls, especially for dessert making. You'll need one very large bowl for beating egg whites and cream.

PASTRY BAGS AND TIPS For this book, you'll need only the basics. Try a simple set of tips to get you started, and find a pastry bag that's a comfortable size for you.

ROLLING PIN Use whatever you have if you feel confident using it. Your grandmother's

pin, a wooden dowel type, or a heavy ball-bearing pin with handles are all terrific.

RUBBER SPATULA One of the great recent advances in kitchen equipment is the availability of heat-resistant rubber spatulas. To be able to use them without worrying about a meltdown is quite wonderful. So now, in addition to scraping down bowls with a spatula while mixing, you can also use it for cooking. Very handy.

STRAINERS I use them often to strain out lemon zest, tiny bits of overcooked egg, and whatever else might get in the way of the perfect smoothness of the final dessert. Have a few on hand, large and small, coarse and fine. A small strainer is perfect for sifting confectioners' sugar over finished desserts just before serving.

SIFTER I sift, but I don't use a sifter; I use a strainer instead because it's faster, and easier to wash. Use whatever you like but for the best crumb, don't skip the sifting step.

TOOLS FOR JUICING LEMONS For squeezing lemons, use either high-tech or low-tech tools. The lowest of low-tech is probably slicing a lemon in half crosswise and inserting a *fork* while squeezing the lemon over a bowl to catch the juice. Nothing wrong with that. Slightly more complex, the beech wood *reamer*, or juicer, is a cone-shaped, ribbed tool that releases the juice when the cut fruit is pressed down and rotated atop the cone. Other low-tech options are the classic 1950s *glass lemon juicers* with a bowl, and plastic or stainless steel *juicers with removable bottoms*. A *lemon trumpet*, available from kitchenware shops and through the Williams-Sonoma catalog (800-541-2233) allows you to extract just the amount of citrus juice you need, without slicing the fruit. Simply twist it into the lemon and squeeze; the seeds are strained automatically, and the juice flows freely through the tube. You can even store the lemon in the refrigerator with the trumpet still in place, until you need juice again. It's made of nonreactive stainless steel and is dishwasher-safe. "Higher tech," heavy-duty, *pump-style juice squeezers* allow you to bring strong pressure on lemons and extract the maximum amount of juice available. The most technologically advanced juicers are *electric juicers*—great to have when you need the juice of many lemons. Feel free to use whatever is on hand.

TOOLS FOR ZESTING The *Microplane* grater's razor-sharp teeth shave a lemon instead of ripping and shredding it. This removes a lot more of the zest than other graters and gadgets; you get at least a tablespoon of zest from each lemon. A Microplane seems to never remove the white pith, which is a minor miracle in itself; all that bitter white pith can ruin a luscious lemon dessert. This tool is very comfortable to hold and use, with a molded rubber handle and a well-balanced shape, like a good knife. I used a Microplane grater for each and every recipe in this book that requires grated lemon zest. Once my lovely friend Marie gave one to me, I was forever finished with all other ways of finely grating zest. Just stroke the lemon across the Microplane as if you were playing the violin; the fine shavings are easy to collect and measure. It's stainless steel, easy to clean, and dishwasher-safe, and produces fine, fluffy wisps of zest. It's not perfect, and it doesn't give you the finest zest possible, however. In order to have perfectly smooth desserts, you will sometimes have to strain out the zest or process it with the sugar in a food processor until it's very finely ground. For information on the Microplane grater, call (800-555-2767) or visit the company's Web site (www.microplane.com). This grater is available through *The Baker's Catalogue* at (800-827-6836) and in many kitchenware shops.

A *zester* is harder and slower to use, and the yield is low, so I rarely use one. A *box grater* tends to keep a good bit of the zest for itself, and you have to turn it inside out and dig for it.

Besides grating, you may also want to remove the zest in long wide strips, which is best done with a *swivel-blade vegetable peeler* or a small sharp knife. Some peelers are sharper than others, and some remove a thicker strip than others. I have one peeler that's great for removing zest and another that fails miserably, taking lots of the white pith with the zest. If that hap-pens to you, remove the pith with a sharp *paring knife*. For long wide strips and julienne strips, remove the zest with a vegetable peeler from stem end to navel end, trim, and use as is or cut into needle-thin strips with a sharp knife.

WHISKS Important and very handy kitchen tools. Try a standard, twelve-inch one that feels well balanced in your hand. I often use a whisk to fluff up the dry ingredients; it's quicker and easier than sifting when sifting is not absolutely necessary. I also use a whisk for folding one component of a dish into another and often find it better than a rubber spatula because the mixture is not as likely to deflate.

WIRE RACK Indispensable for baking. You'll need a couple of large, sturdy racks for cooling baked goods.

let them eat lemon cake

SERVING A HOMEMADE CAKE MAKES ANY occasion special; here are eight marvelous lemon cakes for any and every occasion. There's something feminine about the Mile-High Lemon Angel Food Cake (page 20), and that makes it perfect for an all-girls' birthday party or a bridal shower. More substantial, the Lemon–Olive Oil Chiffon Cake (page 26) would be just right for your favorite guy's birthday dinner; there's nothing frilly about it. I know lots of people who don't love an intense chocolate cake, but have you ever met a soul who doesn't love lemon pound cake? I sure haven't. The Ultimate Lemon Pound Cake (page 24) is perfect for a celebration, or when you just need something wonderful in your life. The Easy Lemon-Almond Cake (page 31) makes any weeknight dinner a special occasion, and you can serve it with fruit or berries in season. The Lemon Pudding Cake (page 23) is a perfect dessert after a heavy winter or summer meal—a real treat with a raspberry, blueberry, or strawberry sauce. Whether you're having one or more of your best chums over for tea, or you and Jane Austen are enjoying the day at home, serve the Victorian Lemon–Coriander Seed Cake (page 34). It's just right with a cup in the afternoon, and then you can enjoy it the next morning for breakfast. After an invigorating day of cross-country skiing and a hearty winter meal, the Lemon Upside-Down Cake (page 32) will hit the spot. Got a friend or family member who loves ice cream? The perfect birthday cake would be the crisp and crunchy, tart and tangy Lemon Meringue Ice-Cream Cake (page 29).

mile-high lemon angel food cake with lemon glaze

Although angel food cake probably derives from an English recipe, we think of it as a purely American classic, like strawberry shortcake. This recipe for the most ethereal and lightest cake of all contains no lemon juice and no lemon zest. Instead, I've used a teaspoon of pure lemon oil to give it an intense, vibrant, and wonderful lemon flavor. The cake is better the day after it's made, so I recommend you plan accordingly. Serve it topped with Lemon Glaze, and consider serving it with Lemon Curd (page 130) and sliced fresh strawberries, Blueberry Sauce (page 136) and Lemon Sorbet (page 119), or Lemon Whipped Cream (page 131). You might even want to try it lightly toasted for breakfast; it's delicious. You'll have fourteen egg yolks left over, so why not make a double batch of Lemon Curd? To have it on hand is one of life's great luxuries. This recipe uses approximately 1 lemon. **SERVES 8 TO 10**

1 cup cake flour (not self-rising), sifted
¾ cup confectioners' sugar
14 large egg whites at room temperature
1½ teaspoons cream of tartar
¼ teaspoon salt
¾ cup granulated sugar
2 teaspoons pure vanilla extract
1 teaspoon pure lemon oil (see page 13)
Lemon Glaze (recipe follows)

1. Position a rack in the middle of the oven and preheat the oven to 375°F. Have ready an ungreased 10-inch tube pan.

2. Sift the flour and the confectioners' sugar together into a medium bowl.

3. Beat the egg whites with an electric mixer on medium speed in a large bowl until foamy. Increase the speed to medium-high, add the cream of tartar and salt, and beat just until the egg whites form soft peaks. Add the granulated sugar, about 1 tablespoon at a time, beating well after each addition, and beat just until the whites form stiff peaks. Add the vanilla and lemon oil and beat until well combined.

4. Sift one quarter of the flour mixture over the egg whites and fold in with a whisk or a rubber spatula. Continue gently folding, one quarter at a time, until all the flour mixture has been added, being careful not to overmix.

CONTINUED ▶

5. Transfer the batter to the pan. Run a table knife through the batter to remove any large air pockets, and smooth the top with a rubber spatula. Bake for 35 to 40 minutes, until the top is golden brown and the cake pulls away from the side of the pan. Turn the pan upside down, and balance it on its elongated neck or pan legs (it if has them), or hang the tube upside down from the neck of a tall bottle. Let cool to room temperature.

6. Turn the pan right side up. Run a knife around the outside edge of the cake and between the cake and the tube. Top the cake with a flat plate, invert it, give a sharp downward rap to the pan to dislodge the cake, and lift off the pan. If the pan bottom is removable, slide a knife between the pan bottom and the cake to release it.

7. Make the glaze. Pour it over the cake and let stand for at least 10 minutes, or until the glaze is set.

8. Use a sharp serrated knife to cut the cake into wedges. (The cake will keep, double wrapped, for 3 days at room temperature and for 2 weeks in the freezer.)

lemon glaze

1 cup confectioners' sugar
2 tablespoons fresh lemon juice
1½ teaspoons finely grated lemon zest
Pinch of salt

Stir the ingredients together in a small bowl. Let stand for 10 minutes before using.

lemon pudding cake

Didn't your grandmother make this? Maybe you knew it as "Lemon Dainty"? This delicate dessert is like a soufflé with its own sauce, but this soufflé doesn't fall. It tastes best warm and is especially good served with Strawberry Sauce or Raspberry Sauce (page 138) or, if you're feeling extravagant, sweetened softly whipped cream. This recipe uses approximately 2 lemons. **SERVES 6 TO 8**

¼ cup (½ stick) unsalted butter at room temperature
1 cup granulated sugar
1 tablespoon finely grated lemon zest
3 large eggs, separated
¼ cup fresh lemon juice
⅓ cup all-purpose flour
One 8-ounce container sour cream
¼ teaspoon salt
Confectioners' sugar for dusting

1. Position a rack in the middle of the oven and preheat the oven to 350°F. Butter a 1-quart soufflé dish. Have ready a 9-by-13-inch baking pan. Put on a kettle of water to boil for the water bath.

2. Beat the butter with an electric mixer on medium speed in a medium bowl until light and fluffy. Add the granulated sugar and the zest and beat until combined well. Add the egg yolks, one at a time, beating well after each addition. Reduce the speed to low, add half of the lemon juice, half of the flour, and half of the sour cream, and beat just until smooth; repeat with the remaining lemon juice, flour, and sour cream.

3. Beat the egg whites with clean beaters on medium speed in a large clean bowl until foamy. Increase the speed to medium-high, add the salt, and continue beating just to stiff peaks.

4. Add one quarter of the whites to the lemon mixture and fold in using a whisk or a rubber spatula; continue to gently fold one quarter at a time until all the egg white mixture has been added; being careful not to overmix. Transfer the mixture to the prepared soufflé dish. Place the 9-by-13-inch baking pan in the oven, set the soufflé dish inside it, and fill the pan with boiling water to a depth of 1 inch.

5. Bake the cake for 1 hour, or until the top is golden brown, the center is just set, and the top springs back lightly when touched. Let cool on a wire rack for 10 to 15 minutes.

6. Just before serving, lightly sift the confectioners' sugar over the top and serve the dessert warm, scooping up some of the pudding at the bottom of the dish, beneath the cake.

ultimate lemon pound cake

If I could take just one dessert with me to a desert island, this glazed lemon pound cake would be it. To me it's perfect—moist, finely textured, sweet (but not too sweet), and refreshingly tart. Serve it toasted or plain, winter, summer, spring, or fall. I brush it with lots of the glaze, because everyone knows that's the best part. Feel free to add 3 tablespoons of poppy seeds to the batter, or whatever suits your fancy. Don't skip the double sifting; it gives the cake a fine and flawless crumb. This recipe uses approximately 2 lemons. **SERVES 12**

3½ cups sifted cake flour (not self-rising)
½ teaspoon baking powder
¼ teaspoon salt
1½ cups (3 sticks) unsalted butter at room
    temperature
2¼ cups sugar
6 large eggs
1 cup milk
1 tablespoon plus 2 teaspoons finely grated
    lemon zest
1 teaspoon pure lemon extract
1 teaspoon pure vanilla extract
½ cup fresh lemon juice

1. Position a rack in middle of the oven and preheat the oven to 300°F. Butter and flour a 10-inch (12-cup) Bundt pan.

2. Sift the flour, baking powder, and salt together twice.

3. Beat the butter with an electric mixer on medium speed in a large bowl until light and fluffy. Gradually beat in 1¾ cups of the sugar, about 3 tablespoons at a time, and continue beating until light and fluffy. Add the eggs, one at a time, beating well after each addition. Reduce the speed to low and add the flour mixture alternately with the milk in batches, beginning and ending with the flour. Stir in 1 tablespoon of the zest, the lemon extract, and vanilla.

4. Transfer the batter to the prepared pan and smooth the top with a rubber spatula. Bake for 1½ hours, or until a wooden pick inserted in the center comes out clean. Let cool in the pan on a wire rack for 15 minutes.

5. Meanwhile, bring the remaining ½ cup sugar, 2 teaspoons zest, and the lemon juice to a boil over medium-high heat in a small saucepan, stirring until the sugar has dissolved.

6. Turn the cake out onto the rack and immediately brush the hot syrup over the hot cake. Let cool to room temperature. Serve the cake cut into wedges.

lemon–olive oil chiffon cake with chocolate glaze

I agree with that old saying, "Chiffon cake is an angel food cake that's gone to finishing school." Because of its high water and oil content, it is refreshingly unfussy, and more moist and refined with a melt-in-the-mouth, eggy texture unattainable with other cake formulas. Very simple to make, it is an important cake to have in your repertoire. Chiffon cakes are best made the day before serving, so that the flavor can intensify and mellow. They also freeze well and thaw quickly. Instead of the Chocolate Glaze, try the Lemon Glaze (page 22), or frost the cake with Lemon Whipped Cream (page 131). If you use the whipped cream, make the cake the day before you serve it and chill it overnight before frosting. Olive oil gives the cake a lovely flavor; just make sure to use an oil that's buttery and mellow, not pungent and peppery. Worried about the combination of olive oil and chocolate? Don't. You wouldn't recognize the flavor as olive oil; it just gives the cake an elusive richness, and the chocolate is a luscious addition. This recipe uses approximately 2 lemons.

SERVES 8 TO 10

1¾ cups sugar
½ cup olive oil, preferably mellow extra-virgin
½ cup water
¼ cup fresh lemon juice
5 large egg yolks
1 tablespoon finely grated lemon zest
2 teaspoons pure lemon extract
1 teaspoon pure vanilla extract
2¼ cups sifted cake flour (not self-rising)
1 tablespoon baking powder
½ teaspoon salt
8 large egg whites
½ teaspoon cream of tartar
Chocolate Glaze (recipe follows)

1. Position a rack in the lower third of the oven and preheat the oven to 325°F. Have ready a 10-inch tube pan. If the pan does not have a removable bottom, lightly oil the bottom of the pan, line the bottom with parchment or wax paper cut to fit, and lightly oil the paper.

2. Whisk 1½ cups of the sugar, the olive oil, water, lemon juice, egg yolks, zest, lemon extract, and vanilla together in a medium bowl until smooth. Sift in the flour, baking powder, and salt and whisk just until blended.

3. Beat the egg whites with an electric mixer on medium speed in a large bowl until foamy. Increase the speed to medium-high, add the cream of tartar, and beat just until the egg whites form soft peaks. Add the remaining ¼ cup sugar, about 1 tablespoon at a time, beating well after each addition. Continue beating just until the egg whites form stiff peaks.

4. Add one quarter of the egg white mixture to the egg yolks and sugar mixture and fold in using a whisk or a rubber spatula; continue gently folding one quarter at a time until all the egg white mixture has been added; be careful not to overmix.

5. Transfer the batter to the 10-inch tube pan. Run a table knife through the batter to remove any large air pockets and smooth the top with a rubber spatula.

6. Bake for 65 minutes, or until the cake has pulled away slightly from the side of the pan and a wooden pick inserted in the center comes out clean.

7. Leave the cake in the pan, turn it upside down, and balance it on its elongated neck or pan legs (if it has them), or hang the tube upside down from the neck of a tall bottle. Let cool to room temperature.

8. Turn the pan right side up. Run a knife around the outside edge of the cake and between the cake and the tube. Top the cake with a flat plate, invert it, give a sharp down-ward rap to the pan to dislodge the cake, and lift off the pan. If the pan bottom is removable, slide a knife between the pan bottom and the cake to release it.

9. Make the Chocolate Glaze. Pour the glaze over the cake and let stand for at least 10 minutes, or until the glaze is set.

10. Use a sharp serrated knife to cut the cake into wedges. (The cake is best made the day before glazing and serving. Store, tightly wrapped, at room temperature.)

chocolate glaze

3 tablespoons light corn syrup
2 tablespoons unsalted butter
1 tablespoon finely grated lemon zest
1 tablespoon water
5 ounces bittersweet or semisweet chocolate, finely chopped

Bring the corn syrup, butter, zest, and water to a boil in a heavy medium saucepan over medium-high heat. Remove the pan from the heat and stir in the chocolate, stirring until the chocolate has melted and the mixture is smooth. Strain through a fine strainer into a bowl and let cool slightly before using.

lemon meringue ice-cream cake

Crisp and crumbly meringues combined with smooth and tangy lemon curd and rich lemon ice cream makes a perfectly elegant dessert. It can, and should be made ahead of time: You can make the meringues and the Lemon Curd a day before you plan on assembling the cake, or you can assemble the entire dessert up to a week in advance. You'll need six egg yolks for the curd and six egg whites to make the meringues. Isn't it amazing how things work out sometimes? Please don't try to use wax paper instead of parchment paper here; the meringues will stick. ∾ Wonderful as is, this cake can also be served with seasonal berries or berry sauces, or Sliced Peaches with Lemon Zest (page 131). Although it's not difficult to make, the results are impressive. It's a little messy to assemble, but don't worry; it doesn't have to be perfect. Even if the cake crumbles a bit, it still looks great on the plate. **SERVES** **12**

1½ cups sugar

2 tablespoons cornstarch

6 large egg whites

¼ teaspoon salt

1½ teaspoons pure vanilla extract

4½ cups Creamy Lemon Custard Ice Cream (page 115) or Almost-Instant Lemon Ice Cream (page 117), softened slightly

¾ cup Lemon Curd (page 130) or store-bought lemon curd, chilled

1. Position the oven racks in the top and bottom thirds of the oven and preheat the oven to 300°F. Trace two 8-inch circles on each of 2 sheets of parchment paper (for a total of 4 circles), and place the paper on 2 large baking sheets. Have ready a 10-inch springform pan.

2. Whisk ½ cup of the sugar and the cornstarch together in a small bowl and set aside.

3. Beat the egg whites with an electric mixer on medium speed in a large bowl until foamy. Increase the speed to medium-high, add the salt, and beat just until the egg whites form soft peaks. Add the remaining 1 cup sugar, 1 tablespoon at a time, beating well after each addition. Beat just until the egg whites form stiff peaks. Fold in the reserved sugar and cornstarch mixture and the vanilla.

CONTINUED ►

4. Spoon the meringue onto the paper circles (using about 2 cups for each circle) and smooth it evenly with a spatula. Bake the meringues for 1 hour, or until light golden brown, switching the baking sheets after 30 minutes. Let cool on the baking sheets on wire racks.

5. Remove the parchment paper from the bottoms of the meringues and set aside the least attractive meringue to use as a garnish. Fit 1 meringue into the springform pan. Spread it to the edge with about 1½ cups of the Creamy Lemon Custard Ice Cream and then with about ¼ cup of the Lemon Curd. Top with another meringue, spread with another 1½ cups of the ice cream and ¼ cup of the Lemon Curd. Add 1 more meringue and top with the remaining 1½ cups of ice cream and ¼ cup of Lemon Curd. Crumble the reserved meringue and sprinkle it over the top. Wrap the dessert tightly and freeze for at least 8 hours. (The cake can be removed from the pan, tightly wrapped, and frozen for up to 1 week.)

6. Let the cake soften in the refrigerator for 30 minutes before serving. Serve it cut into wedges.

easy lemon-almond cake

Here's an elegant and sophisticated cake that's easy enough to prepare, even on a weeknight. It's good year-round—I serve it in late summer and early fall with Rosy Plum Sauce (page 137), in winter with lemon ice cream, in summer with Blueberry Sauce (page 136), and in springtime it's perfect with sliced ripe apricots. A heavy-duty mixer is not necessary, but it's useful for beating the almond paste. This recipe uses approximately 1 lemon. **SERVES 8**

1 cup all-purpose flour

1 teaspoon baking powder

¼ teaspoon salt

¼ cup milk

2 tablespoons finely grated lemon zest

1½ teaspoons pure lemon extract

1 teaspoon pure vanilla extract

⅓ cup granulated sugar

⅓ cup packed almond paste at room temperature

¼ cup (½ stick) unsalted butter at room temperature

2 large eggs

Confectioners' sugar for dusting

1. Position a rack in the middle of the oven and preheat the oven to 350°F. Lightly butter an 8-by-1½-inch round cake pan with straight side, line the bottom with parchment or wax paper, and butter and flour the paper.

2. Whisk together the flour, baking powder, and salt in a small bowl.

3. Whisk the milk, zest, lemon extract, and vanilla together in another small bowl.

4. Beat the granulated sugar, almond paste, and butter with an electric mixer on low speed in a large bowl until the mixture begins to come together. Increase the speed to medium and beat, scraping down the side of the bowl, until light and fluffy. Add the eggs, one at a time, beating well after each addition. Reduce the speed to low and add the flour mixture alternately with the milk mixture in batches, beginning and ending with the flour.

5. Transfer the batter to the prepared pan and smooth the top with a rubber spatula. Bake for 30 to 35 minutes, until the cake is golden brown and a wooden pick inserted in the center comes out clean. Let cool on a wire rack for 15 minutes and turn out of the pan onto the rack to cool to room temperature. Remove the parchment paper and invert the cake.

6. Just before serving, lightly sift the confectioners' sugar over the top of the cake.

lemon upside-down cake

Who needs pineapples? I adore this cake; it's a true lemon lover's delight. Perfect in wintertime, it's luscious served warm after a hearty meal, plain or with Lemon Whipped Cream (page 131). You'll want to slice the lemons as thinly as you can; if you have a mandoline or a slicer, this is the perfect time to use it. Otherwise, use your sharpest knife. This recipe uses approximately 5 lemons. **SERVES 8**

2 lemons

¾ cup (1½ sticks) unsalted butter at room temperature

¼ cup packed light brown sugar

1½ cups all-purpose flour

2 teaspoons baking powder

¼ teaspoon salt

1 cup granulated sugar

3 tablespoons finely grated lemon zest

2 large eggs, separated

¼ teaspoon pure vanilla extract

½ cup milk

¼ teaspoon cream of tartar

1. Position a rack in the middle of the oven and preheat the oven to 350°F.

2. Trim the ends from the lemons and cut the fruit into slices ⅛ inch to ¼ inch thick with a very sharp knife or a mandoline; discard any seeds.

3. Melt ¼ cup of the butter with the brown sugar in an ovenproof, nonstick 10-inch skillet over medium heat. Add the lemon slices,

increase the heat to high, and boil, stirring, for 1 minute. Remove the skillet from the heat and arrange the slices in an orderly pattern in the bottom of the skillet.

4. Sift the flour, baking powder, and salt together into a medium bowl.

5. Beat the remaining ½ cup of butter with an electric mixer on medium speed in a large bowl until light and fluffy. Add the granulated sugar and zest and beat, scraping down the side of the bowl until light and fluffy. Add the egg yolks and vanilla and beat just until blended. Reduce the speed to low and add the flour mixture alternately with the milk, scraping down the side of the bowl after each addition and beating just until blended.

6. Beat the egg whites with clean beaters on medium speed in a large clean bowl just until foamy. Increase the speed to medium-high, add the cream of tartar, and beat just until the egg whites form stiff peaks. Add one quarter of the whites to the batter and fold in using a whisk or

CONTINUED ▶

a rubber spatula; continue to gently fold in the whites, one quarter at a time, being careful not to overmix.

7. Pour the batter over the lemon slices and gently smooth the top with a rubber spatula. Bake for 45 to 50 minutes, until the top is golden brown and a wooden pick inserted in the center comes out clean. Let cool in the pan on a wire rack for 10 minutes.

8. Loosen the edge of the cake with a rubber spatula all around, invert it onto a heat-proof serving platter, and leave the pan over the cake for 5 minutes. Remove the pan and serve the cake warm, cut into wedges.

victorian lemon–coriander seed cake

A seed cake is a classic tea cake from the British Isles, still enjoyed today but especially popular during the Victorian era. It's lovely for breakfast or for an afternoon tea or coffee break, or served, thinly sliced, with ice cream and a berry sauce for dessert. Or try it toasted with Lemon Butter (recipe follows), cream cheese, or Lemon Curd (page 130). The coriander adds a lovely, lemonish flavor. This recipe uses approximately 3 lemons.

MAKES 1 LOAF

2 cups all-purpose flour

2 teaspoons baking powder

½ teaspoon salt

½ cup (1 stick) unsalted butter at room temperature

2 tablespoons finely grated lemon zest

1 cup sugar

2 large eggs

2 teaspoon ground coriander

1 teaspoon ground mace

¾ cup milk

½ cup dried currants

2 teaspoons caraway seeds

Lemon Butter (recipe follows, optional)

1. Position a rack in middle of the oven and preheat the oven to 350°F. Butter and flour a 4½-by-8½-inch loaf pan.

2. Sift together the flour, baking powder, and salt into a medium bowl.

3. Beat the butter and zest with an electric mixer on medium speed in a large bowl until light and fluffy. Add the sugar, eggs, coriander, and mace and beat until smooth. Add half of the milk and beat just until blended. Reduce the speed to low, add the flour mixture in two batches, scraping down the side of the bowl, and beat just until blended. Add the remaining milk and beat just until blended. Stir in the currants and the caraway seeds with a rubber spatula. Transfer the mixture to the prepared pan and smooth the top.

4. Bake for 65 to 70 minutes, until a wooden pick inserted in the center comes out clean. Let cool in the pan on a wire rack for 10 minutes and turn out onto the rack to cool to room temperature.

5. Serve, cut into thin slices, with Lemon Butter, if desired. (The tea bread will keep, tightly wrapped, at room temperature for up to 3 days.)

lemon butter

½ cup (1 stick) unsalted butter at room
　　temperature
1 teaspoon confectioners' sugar
1 teaspoon finely grated lemon zest
¼ teaspoon pure vanilla extract

Stir the ingredients together in a small bowl until combined well.

tart pies and tangy tarts

IT'S A SHAME. SO MANY COOKS WHO FEEL confident about most other culinary tasks are terrified by the thought of making pies and tarts. It's the crusts. Making a pastry crust seems strange and confusing when you read about it, but once you do it right, your hands learn, and you won't have to think about it anymore. If you practice and maybe watch someone who's good at it, you can do it. It's chemistry, like all cooking, and the principles are pretty simple. The reward of being able to serve beautiful pies and tarts is one of the great pleasures of the kitchen. Do it for yourself.

The cheesecake crusts are a cinch, of course; they have crumb crusts, except for the splendid Jerry's Summer Cheesecake (page 57), which has no crust at all. The Ethereal Lemon Angel Pie (page 44) uses meringue as a base; it looks like a beautiful spring basket filled with gorgeous ripe berries.

Both the Lemon Curd and Strawberry Sunburst Tart (page 48) and the Perfect Lemon Tart (page 51) have rich, buttery shortbread crusts that are a snap to make and impossible to bungle. You don't have to be precise when adding the fat, and best of all, you don't even

2

have to roll out the crust for the Perfect Lemon Tart; you can just press it into the pan. It looks like something you could get only at the finest patisserie, and it's one of the all-time easiest desserts to make. The crust is like crisp butter. And, oh, the sleek and tart filling; a commercial bakery could not make a better one.

After you've mastered the shortbread crusts, try a pastry crust made in the food processor. The Chocolate Ganache Tart with Lots of Lemon (page 54) is like a big chocolate truffle with a crisp almond crust. It can be made flaw-lessly by your machine. The Lemon Chiffon Tart (page 52) also has almonds in the crust, which gives the pastry a lovely texture, even if it's your first homemade crust. Then try the Sweet and Creamy Lemon Chess Pie (page 42). It has a classic southern pie crust made with vinegar and shortening, wonderful with the simple filling— a jellylike custard made without milk and par-tially thickened with cornmeal. It's one of the most pleasant textures on earth.

Once you get ready to move on to the "real crusts," head right for the most sophisticated, the Tangy Lemon Meringue Tart (page 46). It has a slightly sweet crust flavored with lemon zest, and if you breathe deeply and follow the directions, you'll be fine. The meringue topping is folded right into the filling, and it's sublime. Not only are the crusts simple and easy, the filling of the Triple-Lemon Cheesecake (page 58) is as luscious and creamy as cheesecakes get and the Lemon–Goat Cheese Cheesecake (page 60) is rich, unusual, and very sophisticated. Then try Mom's Lemon Meringue Pie (page 39); the texture of the filling and meringue are so heavenly, that if there's a slight problem with the crust, nobody will care.

mom's lemon meringue pie

Lemon meringue pie is the only American pie that can equal apple pie in popularity. It sure was a favorite in my family. We called it "Lemon Lerangue" with great affection. My mom made a terrific one, and I was always thrilled when I saw it cooling on the counter. I think this pie is always best eaten the same day it's baked, although it's not bad for breakfast the next day. The filling does need to be hot when added to the crust; you can make it ahead of time and gently rewarm it before proceeding with the recipe. The topping is an unusual meringue; the recipe was generously given to me by my great friend (and the best cook in New York) Deborah Mintcheff. It will not shrink or weep, and it will last. This recipe uses approximately 2 lemons. SERVES **8**

PASTRY CRUST

1⅓ cups all-purpose flour

2 teaspoons sugar

½ teaspoon salt

6 tablespoons (¾ stick) chilled unsalted butter, cut into small pieces

3 to 4 tablespoons cold water

FILLING

1 cup sugar

2 tablespoons finely grated lemon zest

1½ cups water

¼ cup cornstarch

¼ teaspoon salt

5 large egg yolks

½ cup fresh lemon juice

¼ cup (½ stick) unsalted butter at room temperature

MERINGUE

½ cup sugar

1 tablespoon plus 1 teaspoon cornstarch

½ cup cold water

4 large egg whites at room temperature

Pinch of salt

1. To make the pastry crust: Whisk together the flour, sugar, and salt in a medium bowl. Cut in the butter with a pastry blender or 2 knives used scissors-fashion, until the mixture resembles coarse crumbs. Sprinkle 1 tablespoon of the water over the flour mixture, stirring gently with a fork to distribute the moisture evenly. Continue adding water until the dough just begins to come together when a small bit is pressed between your fingers; do not overwork the dough. Press the dough together to form a ball and knead lightly. Shape into a disk and refrigerate, wrapped in wax paper, for at least 30 minutes or up to 2 days.

CONTINUED ▶

MOM'S LEMON MERINGUE PIE *continued*

2. At least 25 minutes before baking, position a rack in the middle of the oven and preheat the oven to 425°F.

3. Roll out the dough on a lightly floured surface to a 12- to 13-inch round. Transfer it to a 9-inch glass pie plate and gently press the pastry against the side and bottom of the plate. Trim the edge ¾ inch beyond the edge of the plate, turn it under, and crimp as desired. Prick holes all over the bottom and side with a fork. Press a piece of heavy-duty aluminum foil snugly into the bottom and against the side of the pie shell and fill with uncooked beans or rice. Bake for 12 minutes, remove the beans, and bake the shell for 8 minutes longer, or until light golden brown. Let cool on a wire rack. Reduce the oven temperature to 350°F.

4. To make the filling: Process the sugar and the zest in a food processor until the zest is finely ground. Whisk together the water, sugar mixture, cornstarch, and salt in a medium saucepan. Bring the mixture to a boil over medium-high heat, whisking constantly, and boil for 1 minute, until the mixture is smooth and almost transparent; remove the pan from the heat. Whisk together the egg yolks and lemon juice in a medium bowl. Add ½ cup of the hot cornstarch mixture to the yolk mixture and whisk to blend.

Return the mixture to the saucepan, bring to a boil over medium-high heat, and boil for 1 minute, or until thick. Remove the pan from the heat, pour the filling through a strainer into a bowl, and whisk in the butter. Fill the cooled pie shell with the hot filling.

5. To make the meringue: Whisk together the sugar and cornstarch in a small saucepan. Add the water and bring to a boil, whisking constantly over high heat, and boil for 1 minute, continuing to whisk. Transfer the mixture to a 1-cup glass measure. Beat the egg whites with an electric mixer on medium speed in a clean medium bowl, just until foamy. Increase the speed to medium-high, add the salt, and beat to form soft peaks. Pour in the cornstarch mixture in a fine stream while the beaters are running, and continue beating until stiff peaks are formed.

6. Top the pie filling with the meringue mixture, using a rubber spatula to create a smooth, domed top. Make certain that the meringue seals in the filling by connecting the meringue with the crust all around the pie. Form swirls in the meringue with a small spoon, starting at the top of the dome.

7. Bake for 15 to 17 minutes, or until the meringue is cooked through and golden brown. Let cool on a wire rack. Cut into wedges and serve.

sweet and creamy lemon chess pie

A chess pie is a perfectly simple southern classic. There are several legends about how it got its name. Is "chess" a corruption of the word "cheese"? Did it come from the pie chest they were stored in? Or was it from the reply of a southern cook who, when asked what kind of pie she had just served said, "Jes' pie"? Regardless of which legend is right, you'll sure love the pie. This recipe uses approximately 1 lemon.

SERVES 8

PASTRY CRUST

1 cup plus 2 tablespoons all-purpose flour

1½ teaspoons sugar

½ teaspoon salt

6 tablespoons chilled vegetable shortening

2 tablespoons milk

1½ teaspoons vinegar

FILLING

1 cup sugar

1 tablespoon finely grated lemon zest

4 large eggs

2 tablespoons cornmeal

¼ cup fresh lemon juice

6 tablespoons (¾ stick) unsalted butter, melted

Lemon Whipped Cream (page 131) for serving
(optional)

1. To make the pastry crust: Whisk together the flour, sugar, and salt in a medium bowl. Cut in the shortening with a pastry blender or 2 knives used scissors-fashion, until the shortening resembles small peas. Add the milk and vinegar and stir with a fork just until the dough begins to come together when a small bit is pressed between your fingers; do not overwork the dough. Press the dough together to form a ball and knead lightly. Shape into a disk and refrigerate, wrapped in wax paper, for at least 30 minutes or up to 2 days.

2. At least 25 minutes before baking, position a rack in the middle of the oven and preheat the oven to 400°F. Have ready a 9-inch glass pie plate.

3. Roll out the dough on a lightly floured surface to an 11-inch circle. Transfer the dough to the pie plate and gently press the pastry against the side and bottom of the plate. Turn the edge under and crimp as desired. Prick all over the bottom and side with a fork. Press a piece of heavy-duty aluminum foil snugly into the bottom and against the side of the pastry shell and fill with uncooked beans or rice. Bake for 15 minutes, remove the beans, and cool the shell on a wire rack. Reduce the oven temperature to 350°F.

4. To make the filling: Process the sugar and the zest in a food processor until the zest is finely ground. Beat the eggs, sugar mixture, and cornmeal with an electric mixer on medium speed in a medium bowl just until blended. Add the lemon juice and beat again until blended. Pour in the melted butter in a fine stream while the beaters are running and beat just until blended.

5. Pour the mixture into the pie shell and bake for 40 to 45 minutes, until just set in the center. Turn off the oven, open the oven door, and let the pie sit in the oven for 30 minutes. Serve warm, or refrigerate and serve cold, with Lemon Whipped Cream, if desired.

ethereal lemon angel pie

The meringue looks like a cloud and has a texture that is so delicate, it tastes as if it was made by an angel. Make it easy for yourself and prepare the meringue the night before you plan on serving it; that way, it's an almost-instant dessert, perfect for entertaining. In this recipe the pie is crowned with fresh berries, but feel free to use sliced ripe fruits instead. You can't go wrong with apricots, peaches, nectarines, or plums. **SERVES 8**

4 large egg whites at room temperature
¼ teaspoon cream of tartar
Pinch of salt
1 cup granulated sugar
¾ cup heavy (whipping) cream
1½ cups Lemon Curd (page 130) or store-bought lemon curd, chilled
2 cups mixed fresh ripe berries
Confectioners' sugar for dusting

1. Position a rack in the middle of the oven and preheat the oven to 225°F. Trace a 9-inch circle on a sheet of parchment paper. Place the paper on a baking sheet.

2. Beat the egg whites with an electric mixer on medium speed in a large bowl until foamy. Increase the speed to medium-high, add the cream of tartar and salt, and beat just until the egg whites form soft peaks. Add the granulated sugar, about 2 tablespoons at a time, and continue beating just until stiff peaks are formed.

3. Spoon the meringue into a pastry bag fitted with a large star tip. Starting at the outside edge of the circle traced on the parchment paper, pipe the meringue into a spiral to fill the circle. Holding the pastry bag upright and starting at the outer edge of the meringue, pipe 1 tier of rosettes along the edge to make a rim; then pipe a second tier of rosettes on the shoulders of the first tier. Or, if you don't have a pastry bag, spoon the meringue in a circle, scooping the sides upward to form a rim.

4. Bake for 1 hour, or until the meringue is dry to the touch. Turn off the oven and leave the meringue in the oven for 2 hours. Peel off the paper. Store the meringue, tightly wrapped, if not using immediately.

5. Just before serving, beat the cream with an electric mixer on high speed in a large bowl just until it forms stiff peaks. Beat in the Lemon Curd just until combined well. Spoon the lemon filling into the meringue shell, arrange the berries on top, and lightly sift confectioners' sugar over the berries. Serve immediately.

tangy lemon meringue tart

This looks as if it just came out of a pastry shop window, but it's quite simple to prepare. It's made like a classic French tart: The filling and meringue are folded together before baking, so that the flavors and textures of a lemon meringue pie are all mixed together. It will seem as if there's too little filling, but don't worry; it's just enough. This recipe uses approximately 2 lemons. **SERVES 8**

PASTRY CRUST

1 cup all-purpose flour

3 tablespoons granulated sugar

1 tablespoon finely grated lemon zest

Pinch of salt

6 tablespoons (¾ stick) chilled unsalted butter, cut into small pieces

1 to 2 tablespoons cold water

FILLING

2 large eggs, separated, at room temperature

¼ cup plus 2 tablespoons granulated sugar

⅓ cup plus ½ teaspoon fresh lemon juice

2 tablespoons unsalted butter at room temperature

Confectioners' sugar for dusting

1. To make the pastry crust: Whisk together the flour, granulated sugar, zest, and salt in a medium bowl. Cut in the butter with a pastry blender or 2 knives used scissors-fashion, until the mixture resembles coarse crumbs. Sprinkle 1 tablespoon of the water over the flour mixture, stirring gently with a fork to distribute the moisture evenly. Continue adding water just until the dough begins to come together when a small bit is pressed between your fingers; do not overwork the dough. Press the dough together to form a ball and knead lightly. Shape it into a disk and refrigerate, wrapped in wax paper, for at least 30 minutes or up to 2 days.

2. Meanwhile, make the filling: Beat the egg yolks and 2 tablespoons of the granulated sugar with an electric mixer on high speed in a medium bowl for 10 minutes, or until very thick and pale. Stir in ⅓ cup of the lemon juice. Transfer the mixture to a heavy medium saucepan and add the butter. Cook, stirring constantly, over medium-low heat until the mixture thickens and leaves a path on the back of a wooden spoon when a finger is drawn across it; do not allow the mixture to boil. Pour the filling through a strainer into a bowl, and cool to room temperature. Refrigerate the filling, covered, until you're ready to fill the tart shell. (The filling may be prepared up to 3 days in advance.)

3. At least 25 minutes before baking the shell, position a rack in the middle of the oven and preheat the oven to 375°F. Have ready a 9-inch tart pan with a removable bottom.

4. Roll out the dough on a lightly floured surface to an 11-inch circle. Transfer it to the tart pan and press in the dough with your fingertips to evenly line the bottom and side of the pan. Trim the edge. Prick the pastry all over with a fork. Bake for 15 minutes, or until light golden brown. Let cool on a wire rack.

5. Beat the egg whites with an electric mixer on medium speed in a medium bowl just until foamy. Increase the speed to medium-high, beat in the remaining ¼ cup granulated sugar, about 1 tablespoon at a time, add the remaining ½ teaspoon lemon juice, and beat just until the egg whites form stiff peaks. Fold the egg yolk mixture into the whites and pour into the tart shell.

6. Bake for 15 to 17 minutes, until the filling is puffed and light golden brown. Let cool on a wire rack.

7. Just before serving, lightly sift confectioners' sugar over the top of the tart. Cut into wedges and serve.

lemon curd and strawberry sunburst tart

This elegant tart is festive enough for a very special occasion and easy enough for a relaxed summer week-end. To put it together really quickly, use 1½ cups of store-bought lemon curd freshened with a squeeze of fresh lemon juice and a pinch of zest. The crust is very easy to work with, and it's luscious, like a huge short-bread cookie. I call it a sunburst tart because it looks like a big round sun with points radiating out like the sun's rays. **SERVES 8 TO 10**

2 cups all-purpose flour

¾ cup (1½ sticks) chilled unsalted butter, cut into small pieces

½ cup confectioners' sugar

Pinch of salt

¼ cup sour cream

1 large egg yolk

½ teaspoon pure vanilla extract

1 cup heavy (whipping) cream

1½ cups Lemon Curd (page 130) or store-bought lemon curd, chilled

1½ pints ripe small fresh strawberries, hulled

1. Pulse the flour, butter, sugar, and salt in a food processor until the mixture resembles coarse crumbs. Stir together the sour cream, egg yolk, and vanilla in a small bowl until combined well; add to the flour mixture. Pulse just until the dough begins to come together when a small bit is pressed between your fingers. (Alternatively, the pastry may be made by hand: Whisk the flour, sugar, and salt together in a medium bowl. Cut in the butter with a pastry blender or 2 knives used scissors-fashion, until the mixture resembles coarse crumbs. Whisk together the sour cream, egg yolk, and vanilla in a small bowl. Add the sour cream mixture to the flour mixture and stir with a fork just until the dough begins to come together when a small bit is pressed between your fingers.) Shape the dough into a disk and refrigerate, wrapped in wax paper, for at least 30 minutes or up to 2 days.

2. Place the dough on a sheet of lightly floured wax paper. Top with another piece of wax paper and roll out the dough to a 12-inch circle. Remove the top piece of wax paper, transfer the dough, paper side up, to a large baking sheet, and remove the wax paper. To make the points on the edge of the crust, hold the edge between the thumb and forefinger of one hand and push the dough between them into a point with your other forefinger. Prick the dough all over with a fork and refrigerate for at least 20 minutes or up to 2 days.

3. At least 25 minutes before baking, position a rack in the middle of the oven and preheat the oven to 375°F.

4. Bake the crust for 15 to 18 minutes, until light golden brown. Let cool on the baking sheet, placed on a wire rack.

5. Beat the cream with an electric mixer on medium high speed in a large bowl just until it forms stiff peaks. Fold in the Lemon Curd and spread about 1 cup of the mixture evenly on the tart shell, leaving a 1-inch border around the edge. Spoon the remaining cream mixture into a pastry bag fitted with a large star tip and refrigerate until ready to serve.

6. Arrange the strawberries, points up, and close together over the cream mixture. (The tart may be assembled to this point up to 3 hours in advance and kept covered.) With the cream mixture in the pastry bag, pipe large rosettes between the strawberries and around the edge.

7. Carefully transfer the tart to a large platter with 2 wide spatulas. Cut the tart into wedges and serve.

the perfect lemon tart

I got this recipe from my friend Marie Regusis, a sensational professional baker who got it from our friend Mary Cleaver. When naming it, I considered calling it "The You-Could-Be-in-Paris Lemon Tart," but I couldn't resist using the word "perfect," because to me, it is. It's also really easy to make. After prebaking the crust, look for any cracks that the filling could seep through. Make a paste with about 1 teaspoon of flour and ½ teaspoon of water, and smear it over the cracks with your fingers to seal them. This recipe uses approximately 4 lemons. **SERVES 10**

½ cup (1 stick) unsalted butter
2 tablespoons finely grated lemon zest
1¾ cups all-purpose flour
1¼ cups granulated sugar
2 pinches of salt
6 large eggs
1 cup fresh lemon juice
½ cup heavy (whipping) cream
Confectioners' sugar for dusting

1. Position a rack in the middle of the oven and preheat the oven to 350°F. Have ready an 11-inch tart pan with a removable bottom.

2. Melt the butter in a small saucepan over medium heat, add 1 tablespoon of the zest, and let stand for 5 minutes. Whisk together the flour, ¼ cup of the granulated sugar, and a pinch of salt in a medium bowl. Pour in the butter mixture in a fine stream, stirring with a fork, and continue stirring until the dough begins to come together when a small bit is pressed between your fingers. Transfer the mixture to the tart pan and press it with your fingertips evenly up the side and into

the bottom. Bake for 20 minutes, or until the crust is light golden brown. Let cool on a wire rack while making the filling.

3. Process the remaining 1 cup of granulated sugar and the remaining 1 tablespoon of zest in a food processor until the zest is finely ground.

4. Whisk together the eggs, the sugar and zest mixture, the lemon juice, and another pinch of salt in a medium bowl until smooth.

5. Beat the cream with an electric mixer on medium-high speed in a medium bowl just until it forms soft peaks. Whisk the cream into the egg mixture just until blended.

6. Place a baking sheet in the oven, place the crust on the baking sheet, and pour the filling into the still warm crust. Bake for 25 to 30 minutes, or until the filling is just set in the center. Let the pie cool on a wire rack.

7. Just before serving, generously sift confectioners' sugar over the tart. Cut into wedges and serve.

lemon chiffon tart

Make a crust, dissolve some gelatin, whip some cream, whisk it into lemon curd, and you're finished with this splendid tart. It will look and taste as if it took you all day and vast amounts of time and skill. Don't be afraid of gelatin; it's very easy to work with. **SERVES 8**

PASTRY CRUST

½ cup whole unblanched almonds (about 4 ounces)

1 tablespoon sugar

1¼ cups all-purpose flour

Pinch of salt

6 tablespoons (¾ stick) chilled unsalted butter, cut into small pieces

1 to 2 tablespoons cold water

FILLING

¼ cup cold water

2 teaspoons plain gelatin

1½ cups Lemon Curd (page 130) or store-bought lemon curd at room temperature

1 cup heavy (whipping) cream

1. Position a rack in the middle of the oven and preheat the oven to 350°F. Have ready a 9-inch tart pan with a removable bottom.

2. To make the pastry crust: Toast the almonds on a baking sheet for 10 to 15 minutes, until golden brown. Let cool to room temperature. Process the almonds with the sugar in a food processor until the almonds are finely ground.

3. Whisk together the flour, almond mixture, and salt in a medium bowl. Cut in the butter with a pastry blender or 2 knives used scissors-fashion, until the mixture resembles coarse crumbs. Sprinkle 1 tablespoon of the water over the flour mixture, stirring gently with a fork to distribute the moisture evenly. Continue adding water just until the dough begins to come together when a small bit is pressed between your fingers; do not overwork the dough. Press the dough together to form a ball and knead lightly. Shape it into a disk. Roll out the dough on a lightly floured surface to an 11-inch circle.

Transfer to the tart pan and press in the dough with your fingertips to evenly line the side and bottom of the pan. Trim the edge. Refrigerate for 20 minutes.

4. Press a piece of heavy-duty aluminum foil snugly into the bottom and around the side of the pastry shell and fill with uncooked beans or rice. Bake for 20 minutes, remove the beans, and bake the shell for 20 minutes longer, or until golden brown. Let cool on a wire rack.

5. To make the filling: Pour the water into a small bowl, sprinkle the gelatin over the water, and let stand about 10 minutes, or until softened. Place the bowl into a larger bowl of hot water, and stir until the gelatin has dissolved and the liquid is clear. Let cool slightly, pour into a medium bowl, add the Lemon Curd, and whisk just until blended. Let cool to room temperature, whisking occasionally.

6. Beat the cream with an electric mixer on medium-high speed in a large bowl just until it forms stiff peaks. Whisk in the Lemon Curd mixture, in batches, just until combined well. Pour the filling into the shell and refrigerate, loosely covered, until set and thoroughly chilled, at least 3 hours.

7. Let the tart stand for 15 minutes at room temperature before cutting into wedges and serving.

chocolate ganache tart with lots of lemon

Rich, intense, dense, and delicious, this is the sort of dessert you'd expect in a very fancy restaurant. Just before serving, try lightly sifting cocoa over the tart or serve it with lemon ice cream if you'd like. This recipe uses approximately 2 lemons. **SERVES 12**

3 large egg yolks

½ teaspoon pure vanilla extract

½ cup confectioners' sugar

2 tablespoons whole unblanched almonds

¾ cup all-purpose flour

Pinch of salt

5 tablespoons unsalted butter at room
temperature

1 cup heavy (whipping) cream

2 tablespoons finely grated lemon zest

8 ounces bittersweet or semisweet chocolate,
chopped

2 tablespoons fresh lemon juice

1. Stir together 1 egg yolk and the vanilla in a small bowl. Process the sugar and almonds in a food processor until the almonds are finely ground. Add the flour and salt and process just until blended. Add the butter and pulse just until the mixture resembles coarse crumbs. Add the egg yolk mixture and pulse just until the mixture begins to come together when a small bit is pressed between your fingers. Do not over-

process; the mixture should not form a ball. Shape the dough into a disk, wrap in wax paper, and refrigerate for at least 1 hour or up to 2 days.

2. Butter the bottom and side of a 9-inch tart pan with a removable bottom. Roll out the dough on a lightly floured work surface to an 11-inch circle. Transfer to the prepared pan and press in the dough with your fingertips to evenly line the side and bottom of the pan. Trim the edge. Prick the dough all over with a fork. Refrigerate for at least 1 hour.

3. At least 25 minutes before baking, position a rack in the middle of the oven and preheat the oven to 375°F.

4. Bake the pastry shell for 15 minutes, or until golden brown. Let cool on a wire rack.

5. Bring the cream and the zest just to a boil over medium heat in a medium saucepan. Remove the pan from the heat and let stand, covered, for 10 minutes.

CONTINUED ▶

6. Meanwhile, melt the chocolate in a heat-proof bowl set over simmering water, stirring until smooth. Remove the bowl from the heat.

7. Whisk the remaining 2 egg yolks in a medium bowl. Add ½ cup of the cream mixture to the yolks, whisking constantly until combined well. Return the mixture to the saucepan and cook over medium-low heat, stirring constantly, until the custard thickens and leaves a path on the back of a wooden spoon when a finger is drawn across it; do not allow the mixture to boil.

8. Whisk the cream mixture and the lemon juice into the chocolate. Pour the mixture through a strainer into a 4-cup glass measure and whisk until completely smooth. Cool the chocolate mixture to room temperature, pour into the pastry shell, and refrigerate for at least 2 hours or overnight, until set and thoroughly chilled.

9. Let the tart stand at room temperature for 30 minutes before cutting into thin wedges and serving.

jerry's summer cheesecake

This recipe comes from the files of Jerry Goldman, my sweetheart and favorite pastry chef. These sublime individual cheesecakes have a lighter-than-air, richer-than-cream texture and a refreshing, clean flavor. They are perfect for summertime because they require no baking. Serve them as is or with Blackberry Sauce (page 137) or Cherry Sauce (page 140). This recipe uses approximately 2 lemons. **SERVES 6**

2 tablespoons cold water

1 teaspoon plain gelatin

½ cup plus 2 tablespoons sugar

2 tablespoon finely grated lemon zest

2 large egg yolks

3 tablespoons fresh lemon juice

¾ cup heavy (whipping) cream

¼ cup crème fraîche or sour cream

One 3-ounce package cream cheese at room
     temperature

½ cup lemon or plain yogurt

1. Oil six 5-ounce ramekins.

2. Pour the water into a small bowl, sprinkle the gelatin over the water, and let stand about 10 minutes, or until softened. Place the bowl into a larger bowl of hot water and stir until the gelatin has dissolved and the liquid is clear.

3. Process the sugar and the zest in a food processor until the zest is finely ground.

4. Cook the yolks, sugar mixture, and lemon juice over medium-low heat in a medium saucepan, whisking constantly, until the sugar

has dissolved and the mixture is warm to the touch. Remove the pan from the heat and whisk in the gelatin mixture. Let cool to room temperature, whisking frequently.

5. Beat the heavy cream and crème fraîche with an electric mixer on medium-high speed in a large bowl just to soft peaks. Beat the cream cheese with an electric mixer on medium speed in a medium bowl until light and fluffy. Add the yogurt and beat until smooth. Add the cream cheese and yogurt mixture to the cream mixture, beating on medium speed and continuing to beat until smooth.

6. Whisk the yolk mixture into the cream mixture and pour into the ramekins. Refrigerate, loosely covered, for at least 3 hours or up to 1 day, until set and thoroughly chilled.

7. To serve, dip the ramekins, one at a time, into a bowl of hot water for about 5 seconds and then run a table knife around the inside edges. Invert the cheesecakes onto 6 chilled serving plates and serve immediately.

triple-lemon cheesecake

Lemon really adds something wonderful to cheesecake—I'm not interested in one without it. Both the acid of the juice and the zing and pleasant bitterness of the zest cut through all the richness and add an enjoyable edge. This cheesecake looks gorgeous as is, but you can decorate the top with raspberries, small perfect mint sprigs, and/or Crystallized Lemon Peel (page 134). This recipe uses approximately 1 lemon. **SERVES 12**

1½ cups graham cracker crumbs

6 tablespoons (¾ stick) unsalted butter, melted

1 cup sugar

1 tablespoon finely grated lemon zest

Three 8-ounce packages cream cheese at room
    temperature

1 cup sour cream

2 tablespoons fresh lemon juice

3 large eggs

½ cup Lemon Curd (page 130) or store-bought
    lemon curd, chilled

1. Position a rack in the middle of the oven and preheat the oven to 350°F. Butter the bottom and side of a 9-inch springform pan. Have ready a roasting pan. Put on a kettle of water to boil for the water bath.

2. Stir together the crumbs and butter with a fork in a medium bowl until combined well. Press the crumb mixture into the bottom of the pan. Bake for 8 to 10 minutes, or until the crust is set. Let cool on a wire rack. Reduce the oven temperature to 325°F.

3. Process the sugar and the zest in a food processor until the zest is finely ground.

4. Beat the cream cheese in a medium bowl with an electric mixer, beginning on low speed and increasing to medium-high, until light and fluffy. Gradually add the sugar mixture, scraping down the side of the bowl with a rubber spatula, and continue beating until smooth. Add the sour cream and lemon juice and beat until combined well. Add the eggs one at a time, beating well after each addition.

5. Wrap the outside of the springform pan with heavy-duty aluminum foil. Pour the filling into the pan and set it in the roasting pan. Place it in the oven, and carefully pour in enough boiling water to reach halfway up the side of the springform pan.

6. Bake for 70 to 75 minutes, until the center is almost set but still slightly jiggly. Do not overbake; the cheesecake will firm as it cools. Remove the roasting pan from the oven and let the cheesecake cool in the water bath for 15 minutes. Remove from the bath and let cool on a wire rack. Remove the foil. Refrigerate the cheesecake in its pan, loosely covered, for at least 8 hours or overnight, until thoroughly chilled.

7. Run a table knife around the inside edge of the pan and remove the pan's side. Spread the Lemon Curd over the top of the cheesecake. Let stand at room temperature for 20 minutes. Cut into wedges and serve.

lemon–goat cheese cheesecake

Here's a heavenly combination. The tartness of the lemon and the goat cheese combines with the richness of the cream cheese to make an unusual and delectable cheesecake. Use a soft, mild fresh cheese, such as Montrachet; you'll find it in logs in the dairy case of your supermarket, in cheese shops, and in specialty foods stores. This recipe uses approximately 4 lemons. **SERVES 10**

1½ cups graham cracker crumbs

6 tablespoons (¾ stick) unsalted butter, melted

2 cups sugar

¼ cup finely grated lemon zest

1½ pounds soft, mild goat cheese

One 8-ounce package cream cheese

½ cup fresh lemon juice

8 large eggs

1. Position a rack in the middle of the oven and preheat the oven to 350°F. Butter the bottom and side of a 9-inch springform pan. Have ready a roasting pan. Put on a kettle of water to boil for the water bath.

2. Stir the crumbs and the butter together with a fork in a medium bowl until combined well. Press the crumb mixture into the bottom of the pan. Bake for 8 to 10 minutes, until the crust is set. Let cool on a wire rack. Reduce the oven temperature to 325°F.

3. Process the sugar and the zest in a food processor until the zest is finely ground.

4. Beat the goat cheese and the cream cheese with an electric mixer in a medium bowl, beginning on low speed and increasing to medium-high, until light and fluffy. Reduce the speed to medium, add the sugar mixture and the lemon juice, and beat until smooth, scraping down the side of the bowl. Add the eggs one at a time, beating well after each addition.

5. Wrap the outside of the springform pan with heavy-duty aluminum foil. Pour the filling into the pan and set it in the roasting pan. Place it in the oven, and carefully pour in enough boiling water to reach halfway up the side of the spring-form pan.

6. Bake for 1 hour and 30 to 40 minutes, until the center is almost set but still slightly jiggly. Do not overbake; the cheesecake will firm as it cools. Remove the roasting pan from the oven and let the cheesecake cool in the water bath for 15 minutes. Remove from the bath and let cool on a wire rack. Remove the foil. Refrigerate the cheesecake in its pan, loosely covered, for at least 8 hours or overnight, until thoroughly chilled.

7. Run a table knife around the inside edge of the pan and remove the pan's side. Let the cheesecake stand at room temperature for 20 minutes. Cut into wedges and serve.

puddings, custards, and a soufflé

I ADORE SOFT, CREAMY, SPOONABLE desserts. From the totally simple to the all-dolled-up, they are the most comforting of desserts, making us feel well loved and taken care of. Try My Favorite Lemon Pudding (page 80). It's fresh tasting, creamy and luscious, and very simple to make. The lemon takes it out of the realm of kid stuff and pops it right in the middle of uptown sophistication. Great with berries, fruit, or all by its lonesome. A Lemon-Fennel Crème Caramel (page 72), with or without a touch of fennel seeds for another dimension and added sweetness, is sophisticated and rich—perfect for adults and kids.

Can't travel to Italy tonight for dinner? Too bad. But you can make a heavenly Lemon Panna Cotta (page 65) that will make you feel like you're there, especially if you serve it with just three drops of that fabulous artisanal balsamic vinegar you brought back on your last trip. The French would really like us to believe that crème brûlée is their invention, but it's totally English. That doesn't mean it isn't bliss, and adding a zing of a lemon makes it even better. It may be the consummate custard (see page 70).

Having a dinner party under the stars on a summer night? Serve the Ultimate Lemon Mousse (page 66) with blueberries; it's refresh-

ing after a big dinner, or almost any dinner. Lemony Rice Pudding (page 81) is simple perfection, and among the most comforting desserts of all. They make a great breakfast the next morning, if there's any leftover. Lemon-Caramel Pots de Crème (page 69) has just the right balance of sweet and tart: the wonderful bitter sweetness of caramel and the zest of fresh lemon. Fresh Lemon Gelatin (page 77) is wonderful. Please give it a try; it's what you've been looking for in commercial gelatin desserts but never found—a fresh, zingy flavor. It combines well with so many things—herbs, fruits, berries, liqueurs, and wines. Give the variation with lemoncello and fresh rosemary a try. You'll wonder how you lived your life without the Lemon Mascarpone-Clementine Gratins (page 74). Smooth, rich, lemony, and satisfying, it's a very special dish that can be made ahead, and we

all love those. The Chilled Lemon Soufflé (page 78) may be my favorite recipe in this book. The perfect example of a lemon dessert born of opposites—cream and foam, sweet and sour, tangy lemon and custard.

lemon panna cotta

Panna cotta translates from the Italian as "cooked cream." It's a simple custard without eggs, just the essence of cream. Not at all French, but totally Italian. If you can only get ultra-pasteurized heavy cream, consider whisking ¼ cup of mascarpone cheese into the mixture. Originally a specialty of the Piedmont region, *panna cotta* is now served all over Italy. I've enjoyed it variously topped with a syrup of Trebbiano grapes, an apricot compote, and blueberry sauce; I've eaten it in bowls, from molds, and even sliced from a loaf pan. In Italy the sauce changes according to the seasons (of course!), and so can yours. Try Cherry Sauce (page 140), Blueberry Sauce (page 136), or Raspberry-Plum Sauce (page 140), or serve it with no sauce at all. It's a great make-ahead dessert. This recipe uses approximately 4 lemons. **SERVES 4**

1¾ cups heavy (whipping) cream
1½ teaspoons plain gelatin
⅓ cup sugar
¼ cup finely grated lemon zest
Pinch of salt
3 tablespoons fresh lemon juice

1. Oil four 5-ounce ramekins.

2. Pour ¼ cup of the cream into a small heat-proof bowl, sprinkle the gelatin over the cream, and let stand about 10 minutes, or until softened. Place the bowl in a larger bowl of hot water and stir until the gelatin has dissolved.

3. Meanwhile, bring the remaining 1½ cups of cream, the sugar, zest, and salt just to a boil over medium heat in a medium saucepan. Reduce the heat to low and cook, at a bare simmer, stirring frequently, for 5 minutes. Remove the pan from the heat, add the gelatin mixture and the lemon juice, and stir until smooth. Pour through a fine strainer into a 4-cup glass measure.

4. Divide the cream mixture evenly among the ramekins. Let cool to room temperature. Refrigerate, loosely covered, for at least 3 hours or up to 1 day, until set and thoroughly chilled.

5. To serve, dip the ramekins, one at a time, into a bowl of hot water for about 5 seconds and run a table knife around the edges. Invert the *panna cottas* onto 4 chilled dessert plates and serve immediately.

the ultimate lemon mousse

Exquisitely simple, this dessert is dazzling served in a tall stemmed glass, garnished with a dab of whipped cream and a tiny, perfect candied violet. Or you could top it with a spoonful of Blueberry Sauce (page 136) just before serving, or create a parfait, alternating layers of berries or a berry sauce and the mousse. This recipe uses approximately 3 lemons. **SERVES 4**

2 tablespoons water
1 teaspoon plain gelatin
½ cup (1 stick) unsalted butter
¾ cup sugar
3 tablespoons finely grated lemon zest
½ cup fresh lemon juice
Pinch of salt
6 large egg yolks
¾ cup heavy (whipping) cream

1. Pour the water into a small bowl, sprinkle the gelatin over the water, and let stand about 10 minutes, or until softened. Place the bowl in a larger bowl of hot water, and stir until the gelatin has dissolved and the liquid is clear.

2. Meanwhile, melt the butter in a large heavy saucepan over medium-low heat. Remove the pan from the heat and whisk in the sugar, zest, lemon juice, and salt. Whisk in the yolks until smooth. Cook the mixture, stirring constantly, until it thickens and leaves a path on the back of a wooden spoon when a finger is drawn across it; do not allow the mixture to boil.

3. Remove the pan from the heat, stir in the gelatin mixture, and immediately pour through a strainer into a bowl. Let cool to room temperature, whisking occasionally.

4. Beat the cream with an electric mixer on high speed in a large bowl just until the cream forms stiff peaks. Add the cream to the lemon mixture in 3 batches, gently folding it in with a whisk or a rubber spatula just until blended.

5. Divide the mousse evenly between 4 stemmed glasses. Refrigerate, loosely covered, for at least 2 hours or up to 2 days, until set and thoroughly chilled.

lemon-caramel
pots de crème

Pot de crème (POH duh-KREHM) is a custard traditionally baked in tiny cups with lids to keep a skin from forming on it as it cooks. Unlike crème caramel, where the caramel lines the baking dish, or crème brûlée, where it's a topping, the caramel in this dessert is stirred right into the custard. You could add a finely chopped lemongrass stalk to the heavy cream as it steeps with the zest. Or maybe you'd prefer chopped crystallized ginger; try about 3 tablespoons. Regardless of the variation, consider serving these luscious custards with Crisp Lemon Wafers (page 103). This recipe uses approximately 1 lemon. **SERVES 4**

1½ cups heavy (whipping) cream
¼ cup finely grated lemon zest
1 teaspoon whole coriander seeds
¾ cup sugar
¼ cup water
6 large egg yolks
¼ cup fresh lemon juice
Pinch of salt

1. Position a rack in the middle of the oven and preheat the oven to 325°F. Have ready four 5-ounce ramekins and a 9-by-13-inch baking pan. Put on a kettle of water to boil for the water bath.

2. Bring the cream, zest, and coriander seeds just to a boil over medium heat in a medium saucepan. Remove the pan from the heat, cover, and let stand for 10 minutes.

3. Meanwhile, heat the sugar and water in a heavy medium saucepan over medium heat, stirring, until the sugar dissolves. Increase the heat to high and boil, without stirring, until the sugar turns a deep amber color, occasionally brushing down the sides of the pan with a wet pastry brush and swirling the pan. Carefully whisk in the cream mixture, reduce the heat to low, and cook, stirring, until the caramel dissolves. Remove the pan from the heat.

4. Combine the egg yolks, lemon juice, and salt in a large bowl, stirring with a wooden spoon. Add ½ cup of the cream mixture and stir gently to avoid air bubbles and to combine well. In a slow steady stream, pour in the remaining cream mixture, stirring constantly. Pour through a strainer into a 4-cup glass measure. Let stand for 2 minutes, then remove any foam that rises to the top.

CONTINUED ▶

5. Place the 9-by-13-inch pan in the oven. Divide the custard evenly among the ramekins. Transfer the ramekins to the pan, place it in the oven, and add enough boiling water to the pan to reach halfway up the sides of the ramekins. Loosely cover the pan with aluminum foil to keep a skin from forming on the custards. Bake for about 30 minutes, or until the custards are just set around the edge and still jiggly in the center. Do not overbake; the custards will set as they cool.

6. Remove the pan from the oven and with tongs or an oven mitt, carefully remove the ramekins from the pan. Let cool on a wire rack. Refrigerate, loosely covered, for at least 3 hours or up to 1 day, until thoroughly chilled. Serve chilled without unmolding.

lemon crème brûlée

Crème brûlée (KREHM broo-LAY) is not a French dish; the name is a translation of the original English dessert "burnt cream," said to have been invented at Trinity College in Cambridge. (But have you ever seen burnt cream on a restaurant menu? As restaurateurs are well aware, many things sound better in French.) This is a luxuriously rich, silky baked custard that's topped with a sheer, crackly layer of caramelized sugar. No wonder it has been called "custard's leap to immortality." The lemon flavor complements and enhances the crème brûlée, but in no way overpowers the subtle vanilla custard. When caramelizing the top, make sure the layer of sugar is as even as possible. Since dark, spotty surfaces are crème brûlée's trademark, a few very dark spots are just fine. If you become addicted to this dessert, consider investing in a small blowtorch made for the home kitchen (see page 14). Remember that the size and shape of your ramekins will affect both the time it takes to cook the custard and the proportion of custard to caramelized topping in the finished dessert. You may need a little extra sugar if the ramekins are particularly shallow and wide. This recipe uses approximately 4 lemons. **SERVES 8**

2 cups heavy (whipping) cream
¾ cup half-and-half
¼ cup finely grated lemon zest
6 large egg yolks

⅓ cup plus 3 tablespoons sugar
Pinch of salt
¼ cup fresh lemon juice

1. Position a rack in the middle of the oven and preheat the oven to 300°F. Have ready eight 5-ounce ramekins and a large roasting pan. Put on a kettle of water to boil for the water bath.

2. Bring the heavy cream, half-and-half, and zest just to a boil over medium heat in a medium saucepan. Remove the pan from the heat and let stand, covered, for 10 minutes.

3. Combine the egg yolks, ⅓ cup of the sugar, and the salt in a medium bowl, stirring with a wooden spoon. Add ½ cup of the cream mixture, and stir gently to avoid forming air bubbles and to combine well. Pour in the remaining cream mixture, stirring constantly. Stir in the lemon juice.

4. Pour the custard through a strainer into a 4-cup glass measure. Skim any foam from the top of the custard. Divide the custard evenly among the ramekins, place the ramekins in the roasting pan, and place the pan in the oven. Add enough boiling water to the roasting pan to come halfway up the sides of the ramekins.

5. Bake for 25 to 30 minutes, until the custard is just set around the edge and still jiggly in the center. Do not overbake; the custard will set as it cools. Remove the pan from the oven and let the custard stand in the water bath for 10 minutes. With tongs or a wide spatula, carefully transfer the ramekins to a wire rack and let cool to room

temperature. Refrigerate, loosely covered, for at least 3 hours or up to 2 days, until set and thoroughly chilled.

6. Preheat the broiler. Gently blot the surface of each custard with the tip of a paper towel to remove any condensation. Sift the remaining 3 tablespoons sugar evenly over the tops of the custards. Place the ramekins in the roasting pan, and carefully pour ice water into the roasting pan to come halfway up the side of the ramekins.

7. Broil the custards about 3 inches from the heat for 1 to 3 minutes, until the sugar has melted and turned a dark amber color; carefully move or rotate the dishes if necessary so the sugar caramelizes evenly. Remove from the broiler and cool the custard in the ice water for 5 minutes. Carefully remove the ramekins from the roasting pan. Refrigerate, uncovered, for at least 15 minutes before serving, but no longer than 1 hour, so the topping doesn't soften.

lemon-fennel crème caramel

Crème caramel (KREHM kahr-ah-MEHL) is a baked custard cooked in ramekins or a larger mold that has been lined with caramelized sugar. The fennel seeds are optional, but delightful. They add a sweetness that's better than sugar and complements the lemon perfectly. This recipe uses approximately 4 lemons.

SERVES 8 TO 10

1⅓ cups sugar
¼ cup water
2 cups heavy (whipping) cream
¼ cup finely grated lemon zest
½ teaspoon fennel seeds (optional)
3 large eggs
2 large egg yolks
¼ cup fresh lemon juice
Pinch of salt

1. Position a rack in the middle of the oven and preheat the oven to 325°F. Have ready an 8-by-2-inch round glass baking dish and a 9-by-13-inch baking pan. Put on a kettle of water to boil for the water bath.

2. Heat 1 cup of the sugar and the water in a heavy medium saucepan over medium heat, stirring, until the sugar dissolves. Increase the heat to high and boil, without stirring, until the mixture is a dark amber color, occasionally brushing down the sides of the pan with a wet pastry brush and swirling the pan. Immediately and carefully, pour the caramel into the round baking dish, tilting it to coat the bottom and side evenly. Let stand to cool and harden. (The caramel may be made up to 2 days ahead and refrigerated, covered; return the caramel to room temperature before adding the custard.)

3. Meanwhile, bring the cream, zest, and fennel seeds, if using, just to a boil over medium heat in a medium saucepan. Remove the pan from the heat and let stand, covered, for 10 minutes.

4. Combine the eggs, the yolks, the remaining ⅓ cup of sugar, the lemon juice, and salt in a medium bowl, stirring with a wooden spoon. Add ½ cup of the cream mixture and stir gently to avoid forming air bubbles and to combine well. In a slow steady stream, pour in the remaining cream, stirring constantly. Pour the custard through a strainer into a 4-cup glass measure and then pour it into the round baking dish. Place the baking dish in the 9-by-13-inch pan, place it in the oven, and pour enough boiling water into the pan to reach halfway up the side of the round baking dish.

5. Bake for 35 to 40 minutes, until the custard is just set around the edge and still jiggly in the center. Do not overbake; the custard will set as it cools. Carefully remove the baking dish from the pan and let cool on a wire rack. Refrigerate, loosely covered, for at least 4 hours or up to 2 days, until set and thoroughly chilled.

6. To serve, run a table knife around the edge of the crème caramel and make certain it is loosened. Invert a flat serving plate with a slight lip over the round baking dish, and invert the crème caramel onto the plate.

lemon mascarpone-clementine gratins

I pretty much stole this recipe. I tasted a version of it at the wonderful Al Forno restaurant in Providence, Rhode Island, and then found the recipe in *Cucina Simpatica*, written by the owners of the restaurant, George Germon and Johanne Killeen. Thank you, George and Johanne! Instead of the clementines, feel free to use any fresh berries—raspberries, blackberries, blueberries, or a combination—just use a generous ½ cup of fruit per gratin dish. This recipe uses approximately 6 lemons. **SERVES 4**

1¼ cups milk

⅓ cup finely grated lemon zest

4 large egg yolks

½ cup granulated sugar

¼ cup all-purpose flour

Pinch of salt

3 tablespoons fresh lemon juice

½ cup heavy (whipping) cream

½ cup mascarpone cheese

8 small seedless clementines, peeled and
    separated into segments

2 teaspoons confectioners' sugar

1. Bring the milk and zest just to a boil in a medium saucepan over medium heat. Remove the pan from the heat and let stand, covered, for 10 minutes. Pour the mixture through a strainer into a 2-cup glass measure.

2. Meanwhile, beat the egg yolks with an electric mixer on medium-high speed in a medium bowl until smooth. Add the granulated sugar, about 1 tablespoon at a time, beating well after each addition. Increase the speed to high and beat for about 2 minutes, or until the mixture is thick and pale. Reduce the speed to low, add the flour and salt, and beat just until blended.

3. Add ½ cup of the warm milk mixture to the egg yolk mixture and whisk until blended. In a slow steady stream, add the remaining milk, whisking constantly. Continue whisking until blended. Return the mixture to a clean medium saucepan and cook, whisking over medium-high heat until the mixture comes to a boil. Boil, whisking constantly, for 2 minutes, or until very thick. Immediately transfer the custard to a bowl and stir in the lemon juice. Let cool to room temperature, whisking occasionally.

CONTINUED ▶

4. Beat the cream with an electric mixer on medium-high speed in a medium bowl just until the cream forms soft peaks. Add the mascarpone and beat until combined well. Add the cooled custard and beat until combined well. (Use immediately or refrigerate the mixture for up to 2 days. Bring to room temperature before proceeding with the recipe.)

5. At least 25 minutes before baking, position 1 oven rack in the center of the oven and 1 on the top shelf and preheat the oven to 425°F. Have ready 4 ceramic gratin dishes (each 4½ inches in diameter with a 1-cup capacity) and a large baking sheet.

6. Place the gratin dishes on the baking sheet and pour ¼ cup of the custard into each gratin dish. Evenly divide the clementines among the dishes and top with the remaining custard. Sift the confectioners' sugar over the tops and bake for 5 minutes, or until heated through. Remove the baking sheet from the oven and preheat the broiler.

7. Broil the custards for 2 to 4 minutes, or until they have dark golden brown spots and are bubbling around the edges, moving the dishes to brown evenly and watching carefully so the gratins don't burn. Serve hot.

fresh lemon gelatin

Fresh lemon gelatin is superbly clean tasting and delightful. It's so simple and sublime, it makes you realize just how truly god-awful store-bought gelatin desserts are—artificially flavored and loaded with sugar. I'd love to give this recipe a name to make it sound as good as it looks. How about Lemoncello Jello? Serve it as is, or with a dollop of Lemon Whipped Cream (page 131), or sliced ripe strawberries, or, for a unique variation, try steeping three 6-inch sprigs of fresh rosemary with the zest, sugar, and water mixture. The rosemary won't hit you over the head, but it does add a very pleasant and mysterious dimension. This recipe uses approximately 5 lemons. **SERVES 6**

3¼ cups water

1 cup sugar

¼ cup finely grated lemon zest

3 tablespoons plain gelatin

1¼ cups fresh lemon juice

2 tablespoons lemoncello (see page 14, optional)

1. Lightly oil a 6-cup mold or six 1-cup molds or bowls.

2. Bring 2½ cups of the water, the sugar, and zest just to a boil in a medium saucepan over medium-high heat. Remove the pan from the heat and let stand, covered, for 15 minutes.

3. Meanwhile, pour the remaining ¾ cup of water into a small bowl, sprinkle the gelatin over the water, and let stand about 10 minutes, or until softened. Place the bowl in a larger bowl of hot water, and stir until the gelatin has dissolved and the liquid is clear.

4. Add the gelatin mixture to the sugar, water, and zest mixture, and stir until dissolved. Stir in the lemon juice and the lemoncello, if using.

5. Pour the mixture through a strainer into the mold and let cool to room temperature. Refrigerate, covered, for at least 3 hours or up to 5 days, until set and thoroughly chilled.

6. To serve, dip the mold into a bowl of hot water for about 5 seconds and if possible, run a table knife around the inside edge. Invert the mold on a large chilled plate, or, if using individual molds, 6 chilled dessert plates, and serve immediately.

chilled lemon soufflé

This is not the easiest or quickest recipe in this book—but it may be the best. If you'd like a fancy garnish, you have many choices: pipe rosettes of cream or lemon curd around the top, garnish it with paper-thin slices of lemons or candied lemon zest, or sprinkle it with pistachio nuts. Sprigs of mint would be beautiful also. After removing the collar, you can sprinkle the sides with sliced unblanched almonds. This soufflé is a workout for you and your handheld mixer, but you can't use a heavy-duty one because the mixture needs to be beaten over simmering water. You'll need a bowl at least 8 inches deep for this, or you'll be wearing your soufflé on your sleeve. This recipe uses approximately 4 lemons. **SERVES 8**

¼ cup water
1 envelope plain gelatin
1½ cups sugar
¼ cup finely grated lemon zest
6 large eggs, separated, at room temperature
¾ cup plus 2 tablespoons fresh lemon juice
¼ teaspoon salt
1 cup heavy (whipping) cream
Raspberry Sauce (page 138, optional)

1. Wrap a 5-cup soufflé dish with a folded strip of heavy-duty aluminum foil or parchment paper to form a collar. Arrange the collar so that it extends about 3 inches above the rim of the dish, and secure it with tape or string. Lightly oil the dish and the foil. Chill the dish.

2. Pour the water into a small bowl and sprinkle the gelatin over the water. Let stand about 10 minutes, or until softened. Place the bowl in a larger bowl of hot water, and stir until the gelatin has dissolved and the liquid is clear.

3. Meanwhile, process 1 cup of the sugar with the zest in a food processor until the zest is finely ground.

4. Beat the egg yolks, sugar mixture, lemon juice, and salt with an electric mixer on medium speed in a large and deep heat-proof bowl until combined well. Set the bowl over a saucepan filled with 2 inches of simmering water and continue beating for 15 minutes, or until the mixture is very thick and pale. Remove the bowl from the heat. Add the gelatin mixture and continue to beat until the mixture cools to room temperature.

5. Beat the egg whites with clean beaters on medium speed in a large bowl just until foamy. Increase the speed to medium-high, sprinkle in the remaining ½ cup sugar about 1 tablespoon at a time, beating well after each addition, and continue beating just until the egg whites form stiff peaks. Beat the cream with an electric mixer

CONTINUED ▶

on high speed in a large bowl just until stiff peaks are formed.

6. Place the bowl with the lemon and egg yolk mixture in a larger bowl of ice water and whisk just until it begins to thicken and set. Gently fold in the whipped cream, and then fold in the egg whites. Pour into the soufflé dish and smooth the top with a rubber spatula. Refrigerate for at least 3 hours or up to 24 hours, until set and thoroughly chilled.

7. To serve, remove the collar from the soufflé. Present the soufflé at the table and spoon onto dessert plates with the Raspberry Sauce, if desired.

my favorite lemon pudding

Here's a perfect example of how well lemon combines with dairy products and eggs to produce extraordinary results using a simple technique. This easy pudding is silky and tart—one of my favorite combinations. I could eat it every day. This recipe uses approximately 2 lemons. **SERVES 4**

¾ cup sugar

¼ cup cornstarch

2½ cups milk

3 large egg yolks, lightly beaten

2 tablespoons finely grated lemon zest

Pinch of salt

½ cup fresh lemon juice

2 tablespoons unsalted butter at room
    temperature

1. Whisk together the sugar and cornstarch in a medium saucepan. Add the milk and whisk until smooth. Add the egg yolks, zest, and salt and cook over medium heat, stirring frequently at first and constantly toward the end, until thickened.

2. Remove the pan from the heat and stir in the lemon juice and butter. Pour through a strainer into a large serving bowl or 4 individual serving dishes. Let cool to room temperature. Refrigerate, loosely covered, for at least 2 hours or up to 3 days, until set and thoroughly chilled. Serve chilled.

lemony rice pudding

There are times when nothing but rice pudding will do. This one is extraordinary, and all it takes is a couple of tablespoons of lemon zest to make it so. If you like, right before serving, whip ½ cup of heavy cream just until it forms soft peaks, and gently fold it into the pudding. This recipe uses approximately 2 lemons.

SERVES **4** TO **6**

2½ cups water

Pinch of salt

1 cup long-grain white rice (preferably jasmine or basmati)

2 tablespoons finely grated lemon zest

3 cups milk

¼ cup packed light brown sugar

¼ cup granulated sugar

1. Bring the water and the salt to a boil in a heavy medium saucepan over high heat. Add the rice and 1 tablespoon of the zest, reduce the heat to low, cover, and cook for 20 minutes. Remove the pan from the heat and let the rice stand, covered, for 10 minutes.

2. Add the milk, the remaining 1 tablespoon of zest, the brown sugar, and granulated sugar to the rice and bring the mixture just to a boil over medium heat. Reduce the heat to low and cook, stirring frequently, for about 30 minutes, or until the mixture is thick and creamy and the rice is very soft.

3. Spoon the pudding into a serving bowl and let cool to room temperature, stirring occasionally. Refrigerate, loosely covered, for at least 4 hours or overnight, until thoroughly chilled.

4. Let stand at room temperature for 10 minutes before serving.

special favorites

DO YOU HAVE A SPECIAL OCCASION approaching and want a really killer dessert to serve? Here's a smashing collection of special occasion favorites, many of which can be made ahead, so you can enjoy that occasion, too. Have a backyard BBQ, a spring fete, or a summertime birthday coming up? Stick those birthday candles in the luscious All-American Strawberry Short-cake (page 84). There's nothing finer; adding the zing of lemon to the strawberries and the biscuits and serving the shortcake with lemon ice cream make it the best ever. Blueberry Pizza (page 87) is another American confection. With a Sweet Lemon-Ricotta Crust and tiny, fresh, ripe blueberries, with or without lemon ice cream, it's a perfect warm-weather dessert. Enjoy it indoors or out, under your favorite shade tree.

Check out the Profiteroles (page 92), served with Almost-Instant Lemon Ice Cream (page 117) and Warm Lemon-Chocolate Sauce (page 136). Sophisticated, stunning, and direct from France, they are superb, but still easy to prepare. Wait until you taste that luscious pool of chocolate sauce. They've got every texture: crisp layers of phyllo combined with lush lemon cream and sliced fresh strawberries topped by crunchy toasted almonds and a dusting of sugar. Love crepes but think they're too hard to make? Classic Lemon Crêpes (page 90) are easy! Even the first of these crispy crêpes turns out well. The Luscious Lemon and Blueberry Tiramisu (page 94), although good all year, seems to be the perfect dessert to celebrate the arrival of spring.

all-american strawberry shortcake

Strawberries symbolize the delights of spring and summer. The best months to buy strawberries are May and June, and as far as I'm concerned, the best use for them is strawberry shortcake. Use small, really ripe scarlet berries, not the huge ones that are white inside and have no flavor—you know, the berries that have more frequent flier miles than you do. Mashing some of the berries and letting the strawberries stand, mixed with sugar, at room temperature draws out the juices to create a rich syrup. My father called this procedure letting the strawberries "get better," and he just wasn't interested in strawberry shortcake unless some of the berries were mashed. I think adding lemon zest makes the berries "get even better." A scoop of Creamy Lemon Custard Ice Cream (page 115) makes a cool complement, or try Lemon Whipped Cream (page 131) instead. This recipe uses approximately 2 lemons. **SERVES 6**

4 pints small ripe fresh strawberries

¼ cup plus 1 teaspoon granulated sugar, or as needed

1 tablespoon plus 2 teaspoons finely grated lemon zest

¾ cup buttermilk

2¼ cups all-purpose flour

½ cup packed light brown sugar

1½ teaspoons baking powder

1 teaspoon baking soda

¼ teaspoon salt

6 tablespoons (¾ stick) chilled unsalted butter, cut into small pieces

1½ pints Creamy Lemon Custard Ice Cream (page 115) or Almost-Instant Lemon Ice Cream (page 117)

1. Position a rack in the middle of the oven and preheat the oven to 425°F. Lightly butter a large baking sheet.

2. Reserve 6 good-looking strawberries with hulls and stems, if available, for the garnish. Hull and slice the remaining berries. Crush half of the sliced strawberries with a potato masher or fork in a large bowl. Stir in the remaining sliced strawberries, ¼ cup of the granulated sugar, adding more sugar if necessary (depending on the sweetness of the berries), and 2 teaspoons of the lemon zest. Let stand at room temperature.

3. Meanwhile, stir together the buttermilk and the remaining 1 tablespoon of lemon zest in a small bowl.

CONTINUED ▶

4. Whisk together the flour, brown sugar, baking powder, baking soda, and salt in a large bowl; break up any large lumps of brown sugar with your fingers. Cut in the butter with a pastry blender or 2 forks used scissors-fashion, until the mixture resembles coarse crumbs. Stir in the buttermilk mixture with a fork just until blended. Do not overwork the dough, or the shortcakes may become tough. Form the dough into a ball; it will be sticky.

5. Transfer the dough to a floured work surface, flour the top of the dough, and pat it into a 1-inch-thick round about 8 inches in diameter. With a floured 3-inch round cutter, cut out 6 biscuits. You will need to press the scraps of dough together into a ball, flatten it out, and recut it in order to have 6. Transfer the biscuits to the prepared baking sheet and sprinkle with the remaining 1 teaspoon of granulated sugar.

6. Bake the biscuits for 15 minutes, or until golden brown. Let cool slightly on a wire rack.

7. To serve, split each biscuit with a fork, place a bottom half on each of 6 serving plates, and spoon over it a generous portion of berries. Arrange a scoop of the Creamy Lemon Custard Ice Cream on the side and add the biscuit top. Spoon on more berries and drizzle the berry syrup over the dessert. Serve immediately, garnished with the reserved whole berries.

blueberry pizza with a sweet lemon-ricotta crust

Simple to make, fun to eat, and gorgeous—this is definitely a crowd pleaser. The pizza crust will spread about 3 inches while baking, so make certain your baking sheet is large enough. This dessert should only be made with tiny wild blueberries. Don't use those huge, bullet-sized berries; they just don't cook quickly enough. This recipe uses approximately 2 lemons. **SERVES 10 TO 12**

Sweet Lemon-Ricotta Pizza Dough
    (recipe follows)
2½ pints small fresh wild blueberries,
    picked over
3 tablespoons sugar
1 tablespoon finely grated lemon zest
3 pints Creamy Lemon Custard Ice Cream
    (page 115) or Almost-Instant Lemon Ice
    Cream (page 117) for serving (optional)

1. Position a rack in the middle of the oven and preheat the oven to 350°F. Generously butter a large baking sheet.

2. Place the dough on a lightly floured sheet of wax paper. Top with another sheet of wax paper and roll out the dough to a 10-inch circle. Remove the top sheet of paper, transfer the dough, paper side up, to the prepared baking sheet, and remove the remaining sheet of wax paper. Fold in the edge of the dough to make a ½-inch rim.

3. Bake the crust for 15 minutes.

4. Meanwhile, toss 2 pints of the blueberries with the sugar and zest in a medium bowl. Top the warm crust with the blueberry mixture.

5. Bake for another 45 minutes, top with the remaining ½ pint of blueberries, and bake for 10 minutes longer. Remove the pizza from the oven and let cool on the baking sheet on a wire rack for at least 5 minutes.

6. Cut the pizza into wedges and serve warm with the Creamy Lemon Custard Ice Cream, if desired.

CONTINUED ▶

sweet lemon-ricotta pizza dough

1⅓ cups all-purpose flour

½ cup sugar

1 tablespoon baking powder

1 tablespoon finely grated lemon zest

Pinch of salt

⅔ cup ricotta cheese

2 tablespoons chilled unsalted butter, cut into
small pieces

1 large egg yolk

2 teaspoons water

1 teaspoon pure vanilla extract

1. Pulse the flour, sugar, baking powder, zest, and salt in a food processor to blend. Add the ricotta, butter, egg yolk, water, and vanilla and pulse just until the mixture begins to hold together when a small bit is pressed between your fingers. Do not overprocess; the mixture should not form a ball. (Alternatively, the pastry may be made by hand: Whisk the flour, sugar, baking powder, zest, and salt together in a medium bowl. Cut in the butter with a pastry blender or 2 knives used scissors-fashion, until the mixture resembles coarse crumbs. Whisk together the ricotta, egg yolk, water, and vanilla in a small bowl. Add the ricotta mixture to the flour mixture and stir with a fork just until the dough begins to come together when a small bit is pressed between your fingers.)

2. Shape the dough into a disk, and refrigerate, wrapped in wax paper, for at least 2 hours or up to 2 days.

classic lemon crêpes

Crêpes are easy to make. Just give them a try, and you'll see how foolproof they are. Even the first one turns out well with this recipe. Crêpe pans are generally a standard size: use one that measures 6 inches on the bottom, or substitute a nonstick skillet of the same size. A ¼-cup metal measuring cup is handy for pouring batter into the pan. Fill it half full for each crêpe. If you find you have holes in your crêpe, dab with a little batter from the measuring cup to fill them. When it's done, just dump it out on a plate and straighten it out as you're cooking the next crêpe. No need to use wax paper between them; they will not stick together. Remember you only have to cook one side one of each crêpe. You will use between 1 and 2 tablespoons of melted butter for making the crêpes, and 4 teaspoons of butter to cook them after they have been filled. This recipe uses approximately 2 lemons. **SERVES 4**

1 cup all-purpose flour
Pinch of salt
1 large egg, lightly beaten
¾ cup milk
½ cup water
About 4 tablespoons unsalted butter, melted
½ cup plus 3 tablespoons packed light brown
    sugar
1 tablespoon finely grated lemon zest
Lemon wedges for serving

1. Whisk together the flour and salt in a medium bowl. Make a well in the center and add the egg. Gradually whisk in the milk and water and continue whisking until blended. Let the batter rest at room temperature for at least 1 hour, or refrigerated and covered for up to 24 hours.

2. Coat a crêpe pan or a 6-inch nonstick skillet with a thin layer of butter and heat over medium-high heat. Pour in 2 tablespoons of the crêpe batter and quickly tilt the pan to spread the batter evenly, covering the bottom of the pan. Cook for 2 to 3 minutes, until the bottom of the crêpe is golden brown and the edge pulls away from the side of the pan. Transfer the crêpe to a plate and let cool. Repeat with the remaining batter to make a total of 16 crêpes, stacking them on the plate as they are done. (The crêpes can be made in advance and refrigerated or frozen, tightly wrapped. Let them come to room temperature before proceeding with the recipe.)

3. Stir the sugar and zest together in a small bowl. Lay out 8 of the crêpes on a work surface and sprinkle evenly with half of the sugar mixture, leaving a 1-inch border around the edges. Fold each crêpe into quarters. Repeat with the remaining 8 crêpes and the remaining sugar mixture.

4. Just before serving, preheat the oven to its lowest setting. Heat 2 teaspoons of butter in a large nonstick skillet over medium-high heat. Arrange 8 crêpes in a single layer and cook for about 2 minutes, or until the bottoms are golden brown and crisp. Turn the crêpes over and cook for 2 minutes more, or until golden brown and crisp. Keep the crêpes warm in a single layer in

the oven and repeat with the remaining 2 teaspoons of butter and the remaining crêpes.

5. To serve, arrange 4 crêpes and some of the butter sauce from the pan on each of 4 warm dessert plates. Serve hot with lemon wedges.

profiteroles

This is a supremely sophisticated dessert—perfect for any grand occasion. Warm lemon-chocolate sauce poured over chocolate profiteroles with lemon ice cream highlights the natural affinity between bittersweet chocolate and lemon. **SERVES 4**

½ cup all-purpose flour
2 tablespoons unsweetened cocoa powder
6 tablespoons water
3 tablespoons unsalted butter
1 tablespoon granulated sugar
Pinch of salt
2 large eggs
¾ cup Creamy Lemon Custard Ice Cream
      (page 115) or Almost-Instant Lemon Ice
      Cream (page 117)
Confectioners' sugar for dusting
Warm Lemon-Chocolate Sauce (page 136)

1. Position a rack in the middle of the oven and preheat the oven to 400°F. Butter a large baking sheet.

2. Sift together the flour and cocoa powder into a small bowl. Bring the water, butter, granulated sugar, and salt to a boil in a heavy medium saucepan over high heat, stirring until the butter is melted. Remove from the heat, add the flour mixture, and stir until the mixture pulls away from the side of the pan, forming a ball. Transfer the mixture to a large bowl, and with an electric mixer on high speed, add the eggs, one at a time, beating well after each addition and scraping down the sides of the bowl. Continue beating until the mixture is smooth and dry looking and has cooled to room temperature.

3. Drop the mixture by rounded tablespoonfuls onto the baking sheet, forming 12 tall mounds and smoothing each one with dampened fingers. Bake for 20 to 25 minutes, until the pastries are puffed and crisp. Let cool on a wire rack. (The profiteroles may be prepared 1 day in advance and stored at room temperature in an airtight container. Reheat the profiteroles on a baking sheet in a preheated 375°F oven for 5 minutes, or until they are crisp, and let them cool on a rack before proceeding with the recipe.)

4. Cut each profiterole in half crosswise with a serrated knife and discard any uncooked dough in the centers. Place about 1 tablespoon of the Lemon Ice Cream between the top and bottom of each profiterole, and lightly sift the confectioners' sugar over the top. Pool about ¼ cup of the Warm Lemon-Chocolate Sauce on each of 4 dessert plates and arrange 3 profiteroles on each plate.

luscious lemon and blueberry tiramisu

I love tiramisu and wanted to make one that shouts "refreshing"; and here it is. So invigorating, it's perfect for a summertime celebration—or the dead of winter, when you wish it were summer. This is so luscious and delightful, you may never go back to a traditional recipe for the Italian confection. This recipe uses approximately 1 lemon. **SERVES 12**

¼ cup sugar

¼ cup water

3 strips lemon zest, removed with a vegetable peeler

One 7-ounce package imported Italian lady-fingers (*savoiardi*)

3 batches Blueberry Sauce (page 136; about 4 cups)

1½ cups Lemon Curd (page 130)

One 8-ounce container mascarpone cheese

½ cup heavy (whipping) cream

1. Bring the sugar, water, and lemon zest to a boil in a medium saucepan over high heat, stirring until the sugar has dissolved. Pour the mixture into a small bowl and cool to room temperature. Discard the lemon zest.

2. Cover the bottom of a 9-by-13-inch glass baking dish with the ladyfingers. Brush them with the cooled sugar syrup. Pour the Blueberry Sauce over the ladyfingers.

3. Whisk together the Lemon Curd, mascarpone, and heavy cream in a medium bowl until smooth. Pour the mixture over the Blueberry Sauce and smooth the top with a rubber spatula. Refrigerate, covered, for at least 6 hours or overnight.

4. Serve in stemmed glasses or bowls.

5

cookies

WOULDN'T IT BE NICE IF WE ALL HAD A full-time cookie baker in the kitchen, ready to whip up a batch whenever a hankering for something sweet and crunchy struck? The world would be a happier place, and we would all get along a lot better. Since it's not a likely scenario, I've made these recipes easy enough to bake on the spur of the moment and sophisticated enough to be shared with my pickiest and most demanding friends. And they are comforting enough that I know I can deal with anything that rears its ugly head after having a treat of cookies and milk.

I love Crisp Lemon Wafers (page 103); I guess that's why my recipe makes 10 dozen. They have a matchless texture and flavor, and can revive my spirit from the doldrums. They are exquisite alone, with ice cream, sliced fresh fruit, mousse, or Fresh Lemon Gelatin (page 77).

Biscotti (page 109) have become very popular in the last few years, and with good reason. They're great anytime of day or night, even for breakfast, and they are the keeping cookie, lasting up to a month. I'm also crazy about pure and simple Old-Fashioned Lemon Sugar Cookies (page 108). It's fun to flatten the dough with a glass before baking. *Langues de chats*, or "cats' tongues" (page 110) are very, very French with a lovely unique texture and a refined, graceful shape. They look terrific stuck in a scoop of ice cream or sorbet or just sitting on the saucer next to a perfect cup of café au lait. Packaged puff pastry is the secret to Easy and Elegant Lemon Straws (page 111). All you need to do is roll out the dough, sprinkle it with lemon sugar, cut it into long thin strips, and twist them as you're placing them on the baking sheet. Pop them in the oven, and Bob's your uncle. The Lemon–

Black Pepper Cornmeal Cookies (page 106) are a sophisticated treat that leaves your mouth just pleasantly warmed. Shortbread is the perfect cookie, simple with a distinct sandy texture that I find irresistible. I love plain shortbread, but lemon takes it to new heights (page 100). Everyone loves lemon bars (page 99)—their crisp bottoms and creamy tops are sweet and tart. Shortbread and Lemon Curd Bars (page 102) are so easy, they're almost cheating. I could go on and on about the World's Best Madeleines (page 104). Their subtle flavor, magic texture, and lovely small size make them, quite possibly, the best cookies on earth. Or are they really little cakes? Give them a try.

I have two nonstick baking sheets, and I use them constantly. They're a battleship gray color—not too dark, so the cookies don't brown faster than they cook, and large enough to make baking a batch worthwhile. I recommend you buy a couple of good quality baking sheets and take good care of them. You'll also need a wide plastic spatula that won't scratch their surfaces. Wash them carefully and keep them at the ready at all times. Some slice-and-bake cookie dough

in the freezer and a clean baking sheet are all you need to have freshly baked cookies often.

I prefer buttering baking sheets rather than smearing them with hydrogenated vegetable shortening; it tastes better, and the butter gives the cookies beautiful brown bottoms. Make sure you let your baking sheets cool between batches of cookies. Remember that using different baking sheets can affect the final cooking time of the cookies, so watch that first batch carefully.

classic lemon bars

Lemon bars, also known as lemon squares, are luscious, tender, melt-in-your-mouth cookies. Serve them anytime. This recipe uses approximately 2 lemons. **MAKES 16 BARS**

1 cup plus 2 tablespoons all-purpose flour

1¾ cups confectioners' sugar, plus additional
    for dusting

2 tablespoons finely grated lemon zest

Pinch of salt

½ cup (1 stick) chilled unsalted butter, cut into
    small pieces

½ teaspoon baking powder

3 large eggs

¼ cup plus 3 tablespoons fresh lemon juice

1. Position a rack in the middle of the oven and preheat the oven to 350°F. Butter an 8-inch square baking pan.

2. Whisk together 1 cup of the flour, ¼ cup of the confectioners' sugar, the zest, and salt in a medium bowl. Cut in the butter with a pastry blender or 2 knives used scissors-fashion, until the mixture resembles coarse crumbs. Knead the dough in the bowl until it begins to come together.

3. Transfer the dough to the baking pan and press it evenly into the bottom. Bake for 25 minutes, or until light golden brown. Let cool on a wire rack while making the filling.

4. Whisk together the remaining 1½ cups of confectioners' sugar, the remaining 2 tablespoons of flour, and the baking powder in a small bowl.

5. Beat the eggs with an electric mixer on high speed in a medium bowl for about 2 minutes, or until tripled in volume. Reduce the speed to low, add the sugar mixture, and beat just until blended, scraping down the side of the bowl. Add the lemon juice and beat just until blended.

6. Pour the lemon mixture over the warm crust and bake for 18 to 20 minutes, until the filling is just set in the center. Let cool in the pan on a wire rack.

7. Just before serving, lightly sift confectioners' sugar over the cookies and cut into 2-inch squares. Store in an airtight container.

buttery lemon shortbread

I remember the first moment I tasted real shortbread; I was captivated. I asked for the recipe and was refused. I've worked on it awhile, and I think this recipe is a lot better than the one my friend's mother wouldn't give to me back in 1966. Cornstarch gives shortbread that almost sandy texture that I find totally irresistible. It is best eaten right out of the oven—and often! This recipe uses approximately 4 lemons.

MAKES 32 SHORTBREADS

2¼ cups all-purpose flour
¼ cup cornstarch
¼ teaspoon salt
½ cup sugar
¼ cup finely grated lemon zest
1 cup (2 sticks) unsalted butter at room
    temperature
1 teaspoon pure lemon oil (see page 13)

1. Position racks in the upper and lower thirds of the oven and preheat the oven to 325°F. Butter 2 large nonstick baking sheets.

2. Whisk together the flour, cornstarch, and salt in a medium bowl.

3. Process the sugar and zest in a food processor until the zest is finely ground.

4. Beat the butter with an electric mixer on medium-high speed in a large bowl until light and fluffy. Add the sugar mixture and the lemon oil and beat until combined well. Reduce the speed to low, add the flour mixture, and beat just until blended; the dough will be crumbly.

5. Knead the dough in the bowl for about 2 minutes, or until it begins to come together when a small bit is pressed between your fingers. Divide the dough into 4 equal pieces. Place 2 of them on each baking sheet and pat each piece into a 5-inch round disk about ½ inch thick. Score the surface of each disk into 8 wedges, using the tines of a fork. Press around the outer edge of each disk with the tines.

6. Bake for 12 minutes, rotate the baking sheets between the upper and lower oven racks, and bake for 12 to 13 minutes longer, until the shortbreads are light golden brown. Remove from the oven and cut through the scored lines. Remove the shortbreads from the baking sheets and let cool slightly on a wire rack. Store in airtight containers.

shortbread and lemon curd bars

These cookies are a combination of two of my all-time favorite things—shortbread and lemon curd. They last longer than you would think, at least 4 days in the refrigerator, and the crust never gets soggy.

MAKES 16 BARS

1 cup all-purpose flour
¼ cup packed dark brown sugar
½ teaspoon salt
½ cup (1 stick) chilled unsalted butter, cut into small pieces
1 cup Lemon Curd (page 130) or store-bought lemon curd, chilled
Confectioners' sugar for dusting

1. Position a rack in the middle of the oven and preheat the oven to 350°F. Have ready an 8-inch square baking pan.

2. Whisk together the flour, brown sugar, and salt in a medium bowl and break up any lumps with your fingers. Cut in the butter with a pastry blender or 2 knives used scissors-fashion, until the mixture resembles coarse crumbs. Knead the dough until it comes together. Transfer the dough to the baking pan and press evenly into the bottom. Bake for 20 minutes, or until light golden brown. Let cool in the pan on a wire rack.

3. Spread the Lemon Curd over the crust. Refrigerate, loosely covered, until ready to serve.

4. Just before serving, lightly sift confectioners' sugar over the Lemon Curd and cut the cookies into 2-inch squares. Store in an airtight container.

crisp lemon wafers

There's very little in this short, sweet life that I love more than a tart, crisp lemon wafer, and these are the very best. When you shape the dough, make two round logs and one with squared-off edges; it will look as if there are two kinds of cookies. Love sandwich cookies? Just before serving, sandwich about 1 teaspoon chilled Lemon Curd (page 130) between 2 cookies. Or for a special treat, try adding 1 tablespoon of fresh thyme leaves and 1 tablespoon of minced crystallized ginger to the dough, along with the egg. This makes a lot of cookies, and it sure is nice to have some frozen ones on hand. This recipe uses approximately 4 lemons.

MAKES ABOUT 10 DOZEN WAFERS

2¾ cups all-purpose flour
1 teaspoon baking soda
1 teaspoon cream of tartar
¼ teaspoon salt
1 cup (2 sticks) unsalted butter at room
    temperature
2 cups confectioners' sugar
¼ cup finely grated lemon zest
1 large egg
¼ cup fresh lemon juice
2 teaspoons pure lemon oil (see page 13)

1. Whisk together the flour, baking soda, cream of tartar, and salt in a medium bowl.

2. Beat the butter, sugar, and zest in a large bowl with an electric mixer, beginning on low speed and gradually increasing to high, until light and fluffy. Reduce the speed to medium, add the egg, lemon juice, and lemon oil, and beat just until blended. Reduce the speed to low, add the flour mixture, and beat just until blended.

3. Divide the dough into thirds; it will be sticky. Transfer one third of the dough to a floured sheet of wax paper and lightly flour the top of the dough. With floured hands, form it into an 11-by-1¼-inch log. Repeat with the remaining dough. Chill, wrapped in wax paper, for at least 2 hours, or until firm. (The dough will keep in the freezer, tightly wrapped for 3 months.)

4. At least 25 minutes before baking, position a rack in the middle of the oven and preheat the oven to 350°F.

5. Cut the dough crosswise into ¼-inch-thick slices and place at least 1 inch apart on 2 ungreased baking sheets.

6. Bake the cookies for 12 to 15 minutes, until the edges are golden brown. Remove from the baking sheets and let cool on a wire rack. Repeat with the remaining dough.

the world's best madeleines

Madeleines are sponge cake–like cookies baked in a special pan with indentations shaped like scallop shells. They were made famous by Marcel Proust in his seven-volume novel *Remembrance of Things Past*. The novel opens with a writer enjoying a madeleine, "This seashell cake so strictly pleated outside and so sensual inside." The little cakes evoked long-forgotten events of his youth and life. Enjoy them with a cup of tea made from lime flowers, as Proust's character did. I have eaten entire batches myself. I once had them for dinner. This recipe uses approximately 2 lemons. **MAKES 1 DOZEN MADELEINES**

¼ cup (½ stick) unsalted butter
2 tablespoons finely grated lemon zest
¼ cup all-purpose flour
¼ cup cake flour (not self-rising)
Pinch of salt
¼ cup granulated sugar
1 large egg
2 large egg yolks
Confectioners' sugar for dusting

1. Position a rack in the lower third of the oven and preheat the oven to 375°F. Generously butter and flour a madeleine mold that makes twelve 3-inch madeleines. Place a dry kitchen towel on a work surface.

2. Melt the butter in a small saucepan over medium heat. Remove the pan from the heat, stir in the lemon zest, and let cool.

3. Whisk the all-purpose flour, cake flour, and salt together in a small bowl.

4. Beat the granulated sugar, egg, and egg yolks with an electric mixer on medium-high speed in a medium bowl for about 10 minutes, or until a slowly dissolving ribbon forms when you lift the beaters. Gently fold in the flour mixture, about 3 tablespoons at a time, with a whisk. Whisk in the butter mixture, about 1 tablespoon at a time, just until blended.

5. Divide the batter evenly among the 12 molds. Bake for 12 to 14 minutes, until the tops are golden brown and the cakes spring back when lightly pressed. Tap one side of the pan to release the madeleines onto the towel and let them cool slightly, flat side down. Serve warm or at room temperature, dusted with confectioners' sugar. Store the completely cool madeleines in an airtight container.

lemon–black pepper cornmeal cookies

The black pepper is not necessary, but it does add interest and a pleasant warmth in the mouth. If you'd rather, add ½ teaspoon of ground ginger with the dry ingredients, instead of the pepper. These are perfect with ice cream and fruit. This recipe uses approximately 4 lemons. **MAKES 6 DOZEN COOKIES**

1¼ cups all-purpose flour

1 cup yellow cornmeal

¾ teaspoon fresh, coarsely ground black pepper (optional)

Pinch of salt

1 cup (2 sticks) unsalted butter, at room temperature

1 cup sugar

¼ cup finely grated lemon zest

2 large egg yolks

1. Whisk the flour, cornmeal, black pepper, if using, and salt together in a medium bowl.

2. Beat the butter, sugar, and zest in a medium bowl with an electric mixer, beginning on low speed and increasing to medium-high speed, until light and fluffy. Add the egg yolks and beat to combine well. Reduce the speed to low, add the flour mixture, and beat on low speed just until blended; the dough will be crumbly.

3. Press the dough together with your hands and divide it in half. Place each half on a sheet of wax paper and form each piece into a 10-by-1¼-inch log. Smooth each log with dampened fingers. Chill the logs, wrapped in wax paper, for at least 3 hours, or until firm.

4. At least 25 minutes before baking, position a rack in the middle of the oven and preheat the oven to 400°F. Butter 2 large nonstick baking sheets.

5. Cut each log into ¼-inch-thick rounds and arrange the rounds 2 inches apart on the baking sheets. Bake, 1 sheet at a time, for 10 minutes, or until the edges of the cookies are golden brown. Transfer the cookies to a wire rack and let cool.

old-fashioned lemon sugar cookies

When I eat these cookies, I feel like I am having a happy childhood right at that moment. Have yours now. This recipe uses approximately 6 lemons. **MAKES 4 DOZEN COOKIES**

1⅔ cups sugar
2 teaspoons pure lemon oil (see page 13)
2½ cups sifted all-purpose flour
½ teaspoon baking soda
¼ teaspoon salt
1 cup (2 sticks) unsalted butter at room
    temperature
⅓ cup finely grated lemon zest
1 large egg
2 tablespoons fresh lemon juice

1. Position a rack in the middle of the oven and preheat the oven to 400°F. Butter 2 large non-stick baking sheets.

2. Stir together ⅔ cup of the sugar and 1 tea-spoon of the lemon oil in a small bowl.

3. Sift together the flour, baking soda, and salt into a medium bowl.

4. Beat the butter, the remaining 1 cup of sugar, the remaining 1 teaspoon of lemon oil, and the zest with an electric mixer on medium-high speed in a large bowl until light and fluffy. Add the egg and beat until well blended. Reduce the speed to low, add the flour mixture and lemon juice, and beat just until blended.

5. Form balls with tablespoonfuls of the dough, roll them in the sugar–lemon oil mixture to coat well, and place them about 3 inches apart on the baking sheets. Flatten each ball with the bottom of a glass until about 2 inches round and ⅜ inch thick. Sprinkle each one with a pinch of the sugar–lemon oil mixture.

6. Bake, 1 sheet at a time, for 8 to 10 minutes, until the edges are lightly browned. Remove the cookies from the baking sheet and let cool on a wire rack.

lemon and anise biscotti

Biscotti simply means "twice cooked" in Italian. The dry crispness and pleasant crunch of these cookies comes from baking the dough twice; it's what makes them last so long, too. In Italy they are often dipped in coffee, Vin Santo (a sweet wine), or even mascarpone cheese. They should be crunchy, but not rock hard. The dough should be soft and sticky; don't be tempted to add too much flour, or the biscotti may be tough. Toasting the anise and almonds makes them more flavorful and keeps the almonds from getting soggy. When you stir them in they will break up a bit, which certainly beats having to chop them. This recipe uses approximately 6 lemons. **MAKES 4 DOZEN BISCOTTI**

¾ cup sliced unblanched almonds or pine nuts
    (6 ounces)
1½ teaspoons aniseed
1 cup sugar
⅓ cup finely grated lemon zest
2 cups all-purpose flour
1½ tablespoons ground coriander
1 teaspoon baking powder
¼ teaspoon salt
¼ cup (½ stick) unsalted butter at room
    temperature
2 large eggs

1. Position a rack in the middle of the oven and preheat the oven to 350°F. Butter 1 large non-stick baking sheet. Have ready 1 ungreased baking sheet.

2. Toast the almonds on the ungreased baking sheet for 10 minutes, or until golden brown.

3. Toast the aniseed in a small skillet, shaking the pan, over medium heat for 3 minutes or until fragrant.

4. Process the sugar and the zest in a food processor until the zest is finely ground.

5. Sift together the flour, coriander, baking powder, and salt into a medium bowl.

6. Beat the butter and the sugar mixture in a medium bowl with an electric mixer, beginning on low speed and increasing to medium-high, until combined well. Add the eggs, one at a time, beating well after each addition. Reduce the speed to low, add the flour mixture and the aniseed, and beat just until blended. Stir in the almonds with a rubber spatula.

7. Halve the dough and place both portions on the buttered baking sheet. Quickly form each piece into a 12-by-1 inch log, and place them at least 3 inches apart on the buttered baking sheet. Smooth the 2 logs with dampened fingers.

CONTINUED ▶

8. Bake for 35 minutes, turning the baking sheet once, or until the logs are golden brown and beginning to crack on top. Let cool on the baking sheet for 10 minutes. Transfer the logs to a cutting board and with a sharp knife, cut each log into ⅜-inch slices. Arrange the slices on the same baking sheet and return to the oven.

9. Bake for about 16 minutes, turning the cookies over halfway through the baking, until crisp and golden brown on both sides. Let cool on a wire rack. Store in an airtight container for up to 1 month.

langues de chats {*cats' tongues*}

Available in all Parisian patisseries worth their sugar, these delicate cookies are terribly refined. They have a slightly grainy texture that's similar to a cat's tongue, a very pleasant sensation on *your* tongue. Not only do they have the feel of a cat's tongue, they are shaped like them as well. Try them, and this will all make sense. This recipe uses approximately 1 lemon. **MAKES 4 DOZEN COOKIES**

¼ cup (½ stick) unsalted butter at room
    temperature
¼ cup sugar
1 tablespoon finely grated lemon zest
⅛ teaspoon pure lemon oil (see page 13)
Pinch of salt
1 large egg white
½ cup all-purpose flour

1. Position a rack on the lowest shelf in the oven and preheat the oven to 425°F. Butter 2 large nonstick baking sheets.

2. Beat the butter, sugar, zest, lemon oil, and salt with an electric mixer on medium-high speed in a medium bowl until light and fluffy. Add the egg white and beat just until blended. Reduce the speed to low, add the flour, and beat just until blended.

3. Spoon the dough into a pastry bag fitted with a ⅜-inch plain tip. Pipe out the dough in 2½-inch-long strips about 2 inches apart on the prepared baking sheets.

4. Bake, 1 sheet at a time, for 4 to 5 minutes, until the edges of the cookies are golden brown. Carefully transfer the cookies with a wide spatula to a wire rack to cool. Repeat with the remaining dough.

easy and elegant lemon straws

These cookies are definitely for grown-ups. They're crisp and nicely caramelized, with the added zing of lemon. Not too sweet, they're perfect with after-dinner espresso or coffee. The better the puff pastry, the better the cookies. If you have access to really good puff pastry (made with butter), as opposed to the regular supermarket variety (made with oil), use it. It's important to cut the cookies evenly so they will bake evenly. Frozen puff pastry is often folded in three places before it's packed in the box; press those divisions back together, or they may haunt you later. This recipe uses approximately 2 lemons. **MAKES 4 DOZEN COOKIES**

½ cup sugar

2 tablespoons finely grated lemon zest

½ teaspoon pure lemon oil (see page 13)

1 sheet frozen puff pastry (half of a 17.3-ounce package), thawed

1. Position racks in the upper and lower thirds of the oven and preheat the oven to 400°F. Have ready 2 large ungreased nonstick baking sheets.

2. Process the sugar and the zest in a food processor until the zest is finely ground. Transfer the mixture to a small bowl and stir in the lemon oil. Let stand for 20 minutes.

3. Lay out a sheet of wax paper on a work surface, sprinkle with half of the sugar mixture, lay the puff pastry on top, and then sprinkle with the remaining sugar mixture.

Cover with another sheet of wax paper. Roll out the puff pastry to a 10-by-12-inch rectangle.

4. Remove the top sheet of wax paper, cut the dough in half lengthwise and then crosswise into ½-inch-wide strips. Twist each strip two or three times, and place about 1 inch apart on the baking sheets.

5. Bake for 6 minutes, rotate the baking sheets between the upper and lower oven racks, and bake for 6 to 8 minutes longer, or until the straws are dark golden brown and the sugar is caramelized. Watch carefully at the end of the baking time; the bottoms can burn quickly. Carefully transfer the cookies with a wide spatula to a wire rack to cool.

6. Serve at room temperature. These are best served the same day they are prepared.

frozen lemon desserts

MAKING YOUR OWN FROZEN DESSERTS is a breeze these days. There are many types of ice-cream freezers available for home kitchens; many of them are small and inexpensive, and they all make fabulous ice cream, sorbet, and frozen yogurt. Homemade frozen desserts are often better than ones made in fancy restaurants, where mixes and frozen purees are often used.

This chapter includes the full gamut of frozen desserts, and there's a good reason for making each one: The rich and luscious Creamy Lemon Custard Ice Cream (page 115) is bursting with heavy cream, egg yolks, and zingy fresh lemon. After you've tried that, move on to the Philadelphia-Style Lemon Ice Cream (page 116), which is made without eggs and really lets the lemon flavor shine through. The Lemon Buttermilk Ice Cream (page 117) is made with nothing but lemon curd and fresh buttermilk

and is refreshing and delightful as it gets. The hearty and satisfying Lemon Ricotta Gelato (page 118) has a touch of cinnamon and the wonderful texture of ricotta cheese. Don't skip the Lemon Granita (page 122); it's a kind of frozen lemonade for grown-ups—simple and invigorating. You'll love the Lemon Sorbet and Lemon Sorbet–Filled Lemons (pages 119 and 120); the sorbet is lightly textured and totally refreshing. The Lemon-Chocolate Sorbet (page 124) combines the rich flavors of bittersweet chocolate and fresh lemon to give you a superb, just-picked taste. To make Almost-Instant Lemon Ice Cream (page 117), you need only stir a few tablespoons of lemon juice and zest into a high-quality store-bought vanilla ice cream. Lemonade Fruit Jewel Popsicles (page 125), a lemonade-based treat with large, shimmering chunks of fresh fruit, will please everyone on a hot summer's day.

some tips for making and storing homemade frozen desserts

Let freshly churned ice cream set in the freezer for an hour or more before eating it. Called ripening, it helps to develop flavors and textures. Chill the container first. Then fill it quickly, and leave a little headroom to allow for expansion. Protect the surface of the ice cream or sorbet with wax paper before snapping on a tight lid.

While ice cream ripens, it also hardens, making it firm enough to scoop. It should be stiff enough to heap into a mound, yet soft enough to be shaken down in the container. If it's too cold and stiff, it will retain air pockets that collect ice crystals, and develop freezer burn. If it's soupy, it will take too long to harden, allowing tiny ice crystals to grow into larger ones, which will create a coarse texture.

Sorbets and most homemade ice cream are best eaten the day they're made. Ice cream made with a cooked custard will hold up longer, up to 10 days. Don't thaw and refreeze ice cream. Ice crystals will develop, and the texture of the ice cream will be unpleasant.

creamy lemon custard ice cream

I have a door on the front of my refrigerator that dispenses ice and water, but I'd much rather it dispense Creamy Lemon Custard Ice Cream. It's perfect with any fruit or berry, sliced or as a sauce. A few crisp cookies are nice on the side. This recipe uses approximately 6 lemons. **MAKES ABOUT 1½ QUARTS**

2 cups heavy (whipping) cream
2 cups half-and-half
1 cup sugar
⅓ cup finely grated lemon zest
6 large egg yolks
Pinch of salt
1 teaspoon pure vanilla extract
¾ cup fresh lemon juice

1. Bring the cream, half-and-half, sugar, and zest just to a boil over medium heat in a heavy medium saucepan, stirring to dissolve the sugar.

2. Whisk the egg yolks and salt together in a medium bowl. Add ½ cup of the cream mixture to the yolk mixture and whisk until blended. In a slow steady stream, add the remaining cream mixture, whisking constantly, and continue whisking until blended. Return the mixture to the saucepan and cook, stirring, over medium-low heat until the custard thickens and leaves a path on the back of a wooden spoon when a finger is drawn across it; do not allow the mixture to boil.

3. Immediately pour the custard through a strainer into a bowl and stir in the vanilla. Let cool to room temperature, whisking occasionally. Refrigerate, covered, for 3 hours, until thoroughly chilled.

4. When ready to freeze, stir the lemon juice into the cold custard, pour the mixture into an ice-cream maker, and freeze according to the manufacturer's instructions. The ice cream will be soft, but ready to eat. For a firmer texture, transfer to a freezer container and freeze for at least 2 hours before serving.

philadelphia-style lemon ice cream

The difference between a custard ice cream and a Philadelphia-style ice cream is about eggs; the Philadelphia style doesn't have any. Their absence gives the ice cream a different texture and flavor—less rich and more refreshing, and the fruit flavor shines through better. It also feels colder on your tongue. This recipe uses approximately 4 lemons. **MAKES 1 SCANT QUART**

2 cups heavy (whipping) cream
1 cup sugar
½ cup plus 2 tablespoons fresh lemon juice
¼ cup finely grated lemon zest
Pinch of salt

1. Whisk all of the ingredients together in a large bowl. Let stand at room temperature for 15 to 30 minutes, whisking occasionally, to allow the sugar to dissolve. Pour through a strainer into a bowl and refrigerate, covered, for 3 hours, or until thoroughly chilled.

2. Pour the mixture into an ice-cream maker and freeze according to the manufacturer's instructions. The ice cream will be soft, but ready to eat. For a firmer texture, transfer to a freezer container and freeze for at least 2 hours before serving.

lemon buttermilk ice cream

Pretty easy, huh? It may be easy, but nothing is more refreshing or clean tasting, or has a tangier flavor. It's wonderful served with Crisp Lemon Wafers (page 103). Don't use unsalted buttermilk; you need the salt for perfectly balanced flavor. **MAKES 1 QUART**

2½ cups chilled buttermilk

1½ cups Lemon Curd (page 130) or store-
   bought lemon curd, chilled

1. Whisk together the buttermilk and Lemon Curd in a medium bowl.

2. Pour the mixture into an ice-cream maker and freeze according to the manufacturer's instructions. The ice cream will be soft, but ready to eat. For a firmer texture, transfer to a freezer container and freeze for at least 2 hours before serving.

almost-instant lemon ice cream

Serve this with a tiny drizzle of Warm Lemon-Chocolate Sauce (page 136), Blueberry Sauce (page 136), sliced strawberries, or a splash of lemoncello (see page 14). This recipe uses approximately 2 lemons. **MAKES 1 GENEROUS PINT**

1 pint best-quality vanilla ice cream, softened

3 tablespoons fresh lemon juice

2 tablespoons finely grated lemon zest

1. Stir all of the ingredients together in a medium bowl until combined well.

2. Transfer the mixture to a freezer container and freeze until firm.

lemon ricotta gelato

I love serving this topped with a fine dice of fresh ripe mangoes and a sprinkling of blackberries, but any fruit or berry sauce would be delightful. Try Cherry Sauce (page 140) or sliced strawberries tossed with sugar and a pinch of lemon zest. The ricotta cheese gives this gelato a wonderful texture. This recipe uses approximately 4 lemons. **MAKES ABOUT 1 QUART**

2½ cups milk

One 15- or 16-ounce container ricotta cheese

½ cup sugar

¼ cup finely grated lemon zest

One 3-inch cinnamon stick

2 tablespoons light corn syrup

1 tablespoon pure lemon extract

1. Bring the milk, ricotta, sugar, zest, and cinnamon stick just to a boil, stirring occasionally, over medium heat in a heavy medium saucepan. Remove the pan from the heat and let stand, covered, for 10 minutes. Whisk in the corn syrup and lemon extract. Pour through a fine strainer into a bowl. Let cool to room temperature. Refrigerate the mixture, covered, for 3 hours, or until thoroughly chilled.

2. Transfer the mixture to an ice-cream maker and freeze according to the manufacturer's instructions. The gelato will be soft, but ready to eat. For a firmer texture, transfer to a freezer container and freeze for at least 2 hours before serving.

lemon sorbet

When it comes to sorbets and other frozen desserts, think of sugar as heat because it lowers a sorbet's freezing point. The more sugar a sorbet contains, the smaller the ice crystals will be, and that mean a smoother sorbet. Too much sugar, and your sorbet will never freeze beyond slushiness; too little, and it will be icy. This recipe has just the right amount. You do need an ice-cream maker for Lemon Sorbet, so it can beat air into the mixture for a light, smooth texture. If you don't have an ice-cream freezer, make the Lemon Granita (page 122) instead. This recipe uses approximately 6 lemons. **MAKES 1 QUART**

1½ cups water
1½ cups sugar
1 tablespoon finely grated lemon zest
1½ cups fresh lemon juice
Pinch of salt

1. Bring the water and sugar just to a boil in a medium saucepan, over medium-high heat, stirring until the sugar has dissolved. Remove the pan from the heat, add the zest, and let stand, covered, for 10 minutes.

2. Pour the syrup through a strainer into a medium bowl and stir in the lemon juice and salt. Let cool to room temperature. Refrigerate the mixture, covered, about 3 hours, or until thoroughly chilled.

3. Transfer the mixture to an ice-cream maker and freeze according to the manufacturer's instructions. The sorbet will be soft, but ready to eat. For a firmer texture, transfer to a freezer container and freeze for at least 2 hours before serving.

lemon sorbet–filled lemons

Who needs those fancy restaurant desserts with feelers bonking you in the head as you try to eat them? To me this is the most beautiful of all dessert presentations. It's stunning in its simplicity, and just looking at it makes you feel refreshed. The hollowed-out lemons may be frozen and kept in the freezer for up to 3 days before being filled with the sorbet, but once you've filled them, they should be served within 12 hours. Freshly made sorbet makes the best filling; the texture is just right. If you make the sorbet earlier in the day, take it out of the freezer and soften it to just-made texture before filling. Select thick-skinned lemons that have not been waxed or otherwise treated, if possible, and if you can find lemons with their leaves attached, grab them. This recipe uses 8 lemons. **SERVES 8**

8 medium lemons

1 quart Lemon Sorbet (page 119) or store-bought lemon sorbet

8 lemon leaves (optional)

1. Cut a lid from the top of each lemon, removing about one quarter of the fruit, and reserve the top. Remove a slice from the base just large enough so the lemon will sit upright; do not cut into the pulp. To hollow out each lemon: Cut into it with a grapefruit-sectioning knife to remove as much of the lemon pulp as possible, leaving the rind intact to form a shell. Reserve the pulp and juice for another use. Freeze the lemon cups and their lids.

2. Spoon the sorbet directly into the frozen lemon cups. Mound the tops generously, add the lids, and freeze for at least 3 hours or up to 12 hours before serving.

3. Just before serving, make a small slit in each lid, and insert the stem of a lemon leaf, if you have one.

lemon granita

Granita is an icy frozen dessert, similar to a snow cone in texture, but with the intense flavor of a well-made sorbet. The ingredients for a granita can be exactly the same as a sorbet's; the only difference is in how they are frozen. A sorbet is churned in an ice-cream maker to keep any large ice crystals from forming, and a granita freezes with only occasional stirring, so that ice crystals will form. I love it, and during the hottest part of the summer, I fantasize about a bathtubful. You may either serve the granita when it has solidified, but is still slightly slushy, or freeze it completely, and then leave it at room temperature for 10 to 20 minutes to soften somewhat before serving. Don't scoop this dessert; serve it by raking along the top with a fork to give a fluffiness to the crystals. A ripe red strawberry or cherry on the stem makes a striking garnish. This recipe uses approximately 4 lemons. **MAKES ABOUT 1 QUART**

2½ cups water
¾ cup sugar
1 cup fresh lemon juice
2 tablespoons finely grated lemon zest
Pinch of salt

1. Place a 9-by-13-inch baking pan in the freezer.

2. Bring the water and sugar to a boil in a medium saucepan over medium-high heat, stirring until the sugar has dissolved. Remove the pan from the heat, add the lemon juice, zest, and salt, and let stand, covered, for 10 minutes. Pour the mixture through a strainer directly into the chilled baking pan. Let cool to room temperature. Cover the pan with aluminum foil and freeze the mixture for 1 hour, or until ice crystals form around the edge.

3. Stir well with a fork to incorporate the ice and return the mixture to the freezer. Stir every 30 minutes for about 2 hours, or until the mixture has become granular but is still slightly slushy.

4. Serve the granita at once, or freeze for 4 more hours, stirring once or twice to break up any large clumps.

lemon-chocolate sorbet

Serve scoops of this intensely delectable dessert garnished simply with raspberries, with maybe a lemon cookie on the side. I make it with good old Hershey's cocoa—nothing fancy. This recipe uses approximately 4 lemons. **MAKES 1 QUART**

2½ cups water
¾ cup packed dark brown sugar
⅔ cup unsweetened cocoa powder
½ cup granulated sugar
¼ cup finely grated lemon zest
2 ounces bittersweet or semisweet chocolate, finely chopped
2 teaspoons pure lemon extract
1 teaspoon pure vanilla extract

1. Bring the water, brown sugar, cocoa, granulated sugar, and zest just to a boil in a large heavy saucepan over medium heat, whisking constantly, until the mixture is smooth and the sugar has dissolved. Increase the heat to medium-high and boil the syrup for 3 minutes.

2. Remove the pan from the heat and let cool for 5 minutes.

3. Add the chocolate to the syrup, whisking until smooth. Pour through a fine strainer into a bowl. Let cool to room temperature. Refrigerate the mixture, covered, for about 3 hours, or until thoroughly chilled.

4. When ready to freeze, stir in the lemon and vanilla extracts, pour the mixture into an ice-cream maker, and freeze according to the manufacturer's instructions. The sorbet will be soft, but ready to eat. For a firmer texture, transfer to a freezer container and freeze for at least 2 hours before serving.

lemonade fruit jewel popsicles

Ostensibly for kids, you'll be surprised how much you and other adults will love these resplendent and refreshing treats. The key to their beauty is simple; just cut the fruit in large enough pieces to reveal what they are, and they'll glow like jewels. **SERVES 12**

6 cups Lemonade (recipe follows) or store-bought lemonade
2 oranges, peeled with a small sharp knife, cut into segments, seeded, and coarsely chopped
16 ripe fresh strawberries, hulled and sliced
½ pint whole small blueberries, picked over
2 kiwi fruits, peeled, halved lengthwise, and sliced thinly crosswise

1. Stir all of the ingredients together in a bowl. Spoon about ¾ cup of the mixture into each of 12 popsicle molds or small paper cups (you may need to vary that amount depending on the size of your molds).

2. Place the tops on the molds or place a wooden stick (like a tongue depressor) or a small plastic spoon into each cup for a handle. Freeze for at least 3 hours, or until frozen solid. (Check the popsicles midway through freezing to make sure that the sticks or spoons are upright.)

3. To serve, remove the molds or tear off the paper cups. (The popsicles can be made up to 1 week ahead and frozen; if you've used paper cups, store the popsicles in resealable plastic bags.)

CONTINUED ▶

lemonade

If you choose to use this as a refreshing beverage rather than as an ingredient in Lemonade Fruit Jewel Popsicles, add 2 cups of cool water with the lemon juice or more to taste, and serve it very cold over ice. This recipe uses approximately 10 lemons. **MAKES ABOUT 6 CUPS**

2⅓ cups water
2⅓ cups sugar
1 lemon, thinly sliced (optional)
2⅓ cups fresh lemon juice

1. Bring the water and sugar to a boil in a medium saucepan over high heat, stirring to dissolve the sugar. Cover and boil for 3 minutes. Remove the saucepan from the heat, add the sliced lemon, if using, and let stand, covered, for 10 minutes.

2. Stir in the lemon juice. Pour the mixture through a strainer into an 8-cup glass measure and discard the lemon slices. Let cool to room temperature. Refrigerate, covered, for at least 2 hours or up to 4 days, or until thoroughly chilled.

confections and sauces

THIS CHAPTER CONTAINS ALL OF THE delectable little sweets and nibbles for serving after meals or using in other desserts. I think of them as life's wonderful little treasures—goodies that belong in tiny jewel boxes and graceful glass bottles. You'll find candies and luscious sauces to accessorize your homemade lemon desserts. Mix and match these accessories, and you'll have an almost infinite number of combinations and permutations. Lemon Curd (page 130) can be used for everything from a spread on toast to a filling for the most worldly tarts. (Not to mention scooped out of the jar with an index finger when you need something sweet, and you need it *now*.) Lemon Whipped Cream (page 131) is great for frosting a cake, serving with strawberry shortcake, pound cake, chess pie, or fresh gelatin. Once you make your own Candied Lemon Peel (page 132), and have it on hand in syrup, crystallized (page 134), or dipped in chocolate (page 134), it just might become a staple in your kitchen. It makes a treat served on the side of coffee, tea, cognac, or whatever. We all love chocolate truffles, but Chocolate Truffles with Lemon Ganache (page 135) are extraordinary. Rich, dark, bittersweet chocolate and fresh lemon are a heavenly combination. You'll also want to try the Warm Lemon-Chocolate Sauce (page 136), great on profiteroles, lemon ice cream, or, in the thinnest drizzle, on a lemon tart.

All of the jewel-toned fruit sauces (pages 136 to 140) are delectable and gorgeous.

lemon curd

Lemon Curd is a luscious, bright yellow, tangy custard made with butter instead of milk. It is like a creamy preserve, only eggs are used instead of pectin as thickening agents. It has a shorter shelf life than preserves, but will last several weeks, tightly covered, in the refrigerator—but only if forgotten. Usually it disappears rapidly, often by the spoonful at midnight. This spread is popular in Great Britain, where it's eaten on toasted bread or cake, on scones fresh out of the oven, in tart fillings, and in trifle. This thick lemon sauce is also excellent over fresh fruit, gingerbread, angel food, or pound cake. My recipe uses only egg yolks and no whites, which makes it much easier to prepare. (You don't have to use a double boiler, which really slows things down.) Lemon Curd is the most useful of pantry staples, and I often make a double batch. This recipe uses approximately 3 lemons. **MAKES ABOUT 1½ CUPS**

½ cup (1 stick) unsalted butter
¾ cup sugar
½ cup fresh lemon juice
3 tablespoons finely grated lemon zest
Pinch of salt
6 large egg yolks

1. Melt the butter in a heavy medium saucepan over medium-low heat.

2. Remove the pan from the heat and whisk in the sugar, lemon juice, zest, and salt. Whisk in the yolks until smooth.

3. Cook the mixture, whisking constantly, until it thickens and leaves a path on the back of a wooden spoon when a finger is drawn across it; do not allow the mixture to boil.

4. Immediately pour the Lemon Curd through a strainer into a bowl. Let cool to room temperature, whisking occasionally. Refrigerate, covered, until ready to serve. (Lemon Curd keeps for a month in the refrigerator and for about 3 months in the freezer.)

lemon whipped cream

This delectable treat has infinite uses. Frost a chiffon or angel food cake with it, or the cake of your choice. It's also good with All-American Strawberry Shortcake (page 84), Blueberry Pizza with a Sweet Lemon-Ricotta Crust (page 87), Classic Lemon Bars (99), Chocolate Ganache Tart with Lots of Lemon (page 54), My Favorite Lemon Pudding (page 80), the Ultimate Lemon Mousse (page 66), Fresh Lemon Gelatin (page 77), Sweet and Creamy Lemon Chess Pie (page 42), and the list goes on. This recipe uses approximately 1 lemon.

MAKES ABOUT 2 CUPS

1 cup heavy (whipping) cream
2 tablespoons confectioners' sugar
1 tablespoon finely grated lemon zest

1. Beat the cream with an electric mixer on high speed in a large bowl just until it forms soft peaks. Add the confectioners' sugar and zest and beat just until stiff peaks are formed.

sliced peaches with lemon zest

Use these tangy peaches instead of strawberries for the All-American Strawberry Shortcake (page 84). This recipe uses approximately 1 lemon. **MAKES ABOUT 4 CUPS**

8 ripe small peaches
½ cup sugar, or to taste, depending on the sweetness of the peaches
2 teaspoons finely grated lemon zest

1. Cook the peaches in a large pot of boiling water for 30 to 60 seconds. Peel, pit, and thinly slice the peaches.

2. Place the peaches in a medium bowl, add the sugar and lemon zest, and stir until combined well.

candied lemon peel

Candied Lemon Peel is great for using in breads, especially panettone or stollen, fruitcakes, muffins, and quick breads. It makes a refreshing and tart nibble as a sweet alongside tea, coffee, cognac, ice cream, or sorbet. Savor it as an after-dinner candy; it seems to magically whisk away the weight of a large meal. Cut into thin ribbons, it's a great garnish for mousse, poached fruits, tarts, and cakes. One of my favorite ways to use Candied Lemon Peel is to dice it finely and add it to homemade apple pie. It also makes a wonderful gift. It does take some time, but mostly it's waiting for the peels to cook. This recipe uses approximately 7 lemons.
MAKES 3 CUPS

6 large lemons
2 cups sugar
2 cups water
½ cup light corn syrup
¼ cup fresh lemon juice
½ teaspoon pure vanilla extract

1. Trim the ends of each lemon with a sharp knife. Cut the lemons lengthwise into quarters. Remove most of the pulp, leaving about ⅛ to ¼ inch of it on each piece of the peel; reserve the rest of the pulp for another use. Cut each strip of peel lengthwise into 3 thin strips.

2. Fill a large saucepan with cool water, add the peel, and bring to a boil; continue boiling for 5 minutes. Drain the peel in a colander, rinse under cold running water, and blanch the peel again, beginning with fresh cool water. Drain in a colander.

3. Bring the sugar, water, corn syrup, lemon juice, and vanilla to a boil in the same saucepan over high heat, stirring until the sugar has dissolved. Boil the syrup for 2 minutes. Reduce the heat to medium-low, add the drained lemon peel, and simmer briskly, stirring frequently to avoid sticking (especially toward the end), for about 1 hour, or until the peel becomes translucent and the sugar syrup thickens. As the liquid reduces, it will go from a brisk simmer to a boil.

4. Remove the pan from the heat and cool the peel in the syrup at room temperature, covered, for at least 3 hours, or overnight. Transfer the syrup and the candied peel to three ½-pint jars, and refrigerate, tightly covered, for up to 1 month.

crystallized lemon peel

MAKES **72** STRIPS

1½ ups sugar
Candied Lemon Peel (page 132)

1. Place the sugar in a medium bowl.

2. Drain the Candied Lemon Peel.

3. Toss the pieces of the drained peel, 1 at a time, with the sugar to coat thoroughly, and shake off the excess.

4. Transfer the peel to wire racks to dry, overnight or up to 2 days. Store the candy in an airtight container with wax paper between the layers. (It keeps for 5 to 7 days.)

NOTE: If, because of humidity in the air, the lemon peel doesn't dry properly, place them in your oven on its lowest setting and bake for 15 to 20 minutes.

chocolate-dipped crystallized lemon peel

MAKES **72** STRIPS

4 ounces bittersweet or semisweet chocolate, chopped
Crystallized Lemon Peel (above)

1. Melt the chocolate in a heat-proof bowl over simmering water, stirring until smooth. Remove the bowl from the heat and let cool slightly.

2. Dip the top one quarter of each strip of Crystallized Lemon Peel into the chocolate and shake off the excess.

3. Transfer the coated peel to wax paper–lined baking sheets and let stand for at least 10 minutes, or until the chocolate has set. These are best eaten the same day they're prepared.

chocolate truffles with lemon ganache

Lemon is a fabulous matchup with bittersweet chocolate, far better than the classic alliance of orange and chocolate. While orange brings only sweetness to the relationship, the lemon, with its complex tart and wonderfully bitter flavor, offers the perfect counterpoint to chocolate's intensity. The lemon in this ganache enhances both the sweet and bitter flavors of chocolate and gives the truffles a clean, just-picked flavor. Truffles are not supposed to be perfectly round; they should resemble the truffle that grows underground. Making these is fun—a little like mud pies for grown-ups. This recipe uses approximately 1 lemon.

MAKES ABOUT 3 DOZEN TRUFFLES

¾ cup heavy (whipping) cream

3 tablespoons unsalted butter

6 ounces bittersweet or semisweet chocolate, chopped

1 tablespoon finely grated lemon zest, or
¼ teaspoon pure lemon oil (see page 13)

¼ cup unsweetened cocoa powder, sifted, for coating

1. Bring the cream and butter just to a boil in a medium saucepan over medium-high heat. Remove the pan from the heat, add the chocolate and lemon zest or oil, and whisk until smooth. (If using the zest, let stand for 10 minutes, covered, and pour the mixture through a strainer into a bowl.) Let cool to room temperature, and refrigerate, covered, for 1 hour, or until firm.

2. Form 1-inch balls with heaping teaspoons of the chocolate mixture and roll in the cocoa powder. Refrigerate the truffles on a baking sheet lined with wax paper for 30 minutes, or until they are firm. Remove from the refrigerator 20 to 30 minutes before serving. (The truffles will keep, refrigerated, in an airtight container for at least 1 week.)

warm lemon-chocolate sauce

This sauce is perfect drizzled over lemon ice cream. You'll need just a little for a very dramatic presentation, especially if you garnish it with fresh raspberries or long-stemmed strawberries. It's also magical drizzled on the Perfect Lemon Tart (page 51), and it's obviously a requirement for the Profiteroles with Lemon Ice Cream and Warm Lemon-Chocolate Sauce (page 92). This recipe uses approximately 1 lemon. **MAKES 1 CUP**

6 ounces bittersweet or semisweet chocolate, finely chopped
¼ cup heavy (whipping) cream
3 tablespoons water
1 tablespoon finely grated lemon zest

1. Melt the chocolate with the cream, water, and zest in a heat-proof bowl set over simmering water, stirring until smooth.

2. Pour the mixture through a fine strainer into a bowl. (The sauce will keep for 1 week, covered, in the refrigerator. Reheat gently.)

blueberry sauce

This recipe uses approximately 1 lemon. **MAKES A SCANT 1½ CUPS**

1 pint fresh blueberries, picked over
⅓ cup confectioners' sugar
2 tablespoons water
1 to 2 teaspoons fresh lemon juice

1. Cook the blueberries, sugar, and water over medium heat, stirring occasionally, in a large saucepan, for 5 minutes, or until the berries are softened and a sauce is formed.

2. Transfer the mixture to a bowl and stir in the lemon juice to taste. Serve warm or cold. Cool to room temperature before refrigerating. (The sauce will keep for 1 week, covered, in the refrigerator. Reheat gently.)

blackberry sauce

This recipe uses approximately 1 lemon. **MAKES A SCANT 2 CUPS**

Three ½-pint containers fresh blackberries,
   picked over
½ to ¾ cup confectioners' sugar, depending
   on the sweetness of the berries
1 to 2 teaspoons fresh lemon juice

1. Puree the blackberries in a food processor. Sift the sugar over the berries and pulse until smooth.

2. Pour through a strainer into a bowl. Stir in the lemon juice to taste. The sauce will thicken on standing; add water, as needed, to thin to desired consistency just before serving. (The sauce will keep for 1 week, covered, in the refrigerator.)

rosy plum sauce

This recipe uses approximately 1 lemon. **MAKES ABOUT 2 CUPS**

6 large ripe purple and/or red plums (about
   1½ pounds), pitted and chopped
4 to 5 tablespoons sugar, depending on the
   sweetness of the plums
2 to 3 teaspoons fresh lemon juice

1. Cook the plums and the sugar in a medium saucepan over medium-low heat, stirring frequently, for 15 to 20 minutes, or until the plums are very soft.

2. Cool the mixture slightly, puree in a food processor, and pour through a fine strainer into a bowl. Stir in the lemon juice to taste. Serve warm or cold. Cool to room temperature before refrigerating. (The sauce will keep for 1 week, covered, in the refrigerator. Reheat gently.)

raspberry sauce

This recipe uses approximately 1 lemon. **MAKES A SCANT 2 CUPS**

Three ½-pint containers ripe fresh raspberries,
    picked over
½ to ¾ cup confectioners' sugar, depending
    on the sweetness of the berries
1 to 2 teaspoons fresh lemon juice

1. Puree the raspberries in a food processor. Sift the sugar over the berries and pulse until smooth.

2. Pour through a strainer into a bowl. Stir in the lemon juice to taste. The sauce will thicken on standing; add water, as needed, to thin to desired consistency just before serving. (The sauce will keep for 1 week, covered, in the refrigerator.)

strawberry sauce

This recipe uses approximately 1 lemon. **MAKES ABOUT 2 CUPS**

2 pints ripe fresh strawberries, hulled and
    sliced
4 to 6 tablespoons light corn syrup, depending
    on the sweetness of the berries
¼ cup water
2 to 3 teaspoons fresh lemon juice

1. Cook the strawberries, corn syrup, and water over medium heat in a large saucepan, stirring occasionally, for 10 minutes, or until the berries are softened and a sauce is formed.

2. Puree the mixture in a food processor and pour through a coarse strainer into a bowl. Stir in the lemon juice to taste. Serve warm or cold. Cool to room temperature before refrigerating. (The sauce will keep for 1 week, covered, in the refrigerator. Reheat gently.)

raspberry-plum sauce

This recipe uses approximately 1 lemon. **MAKES ABOUT 2 CUPS**

4 large ripe purple and/or red plums
   (about 1 pound), pitted and chopped
½ pint ripe fresh raspberries
⅓ cup sugar, or to taste depending on the
   sweetness of the plums
1 to 2 tablespoons water, if necessary
2 to 3 teaspoons fresh lemon juice

1. Cook the plums, raspberries, and sugar over low heat in a medium saucepan, stirring frequently, for about 15 minutes, or until the plums are very soft, adding the water if necessary.

2. Pour the mixture through a strainer into a bowl. Stir in the lemon juice to taste. Serve warm or cold. Cool to room temperature before refrigerating. (The sauce will keep for 1 week, covered, in the refrigerator. Reheat gently.)

cherry sauce

This recipe uses approximately 1 lemon. **MAKES ABOUT 2 CUPS**

2 cups fresh pitted dark sweet cherries
½ cup plus 1 tablespoon water
1 teaspoon cornstarch
3 to 6 tablespoons light corn syrup, depending
   on the sweetness of the cherries
2 to 3 teaspoons fresh lemon juice

1. Cook the cherries in ½ cup of the water in a medium saucepan over medium heat, stirring, for about 10 minutes, or until the cherries are soft.

2. Cool the mixture slightly, puree in a food processor, and pour through a fine strainer into the same clean saucepan.

3. Whisk together the remaining 1 tablespoon of water and the cornstarch in a small bowl. Bring the cherry puree to a boil, whisk in the cornstarch mixture, and boil, whisking constantly, until the sauce is thickened. Whisk in the light corn syrup and the lemon juice to taste. Serve warm or cold. Cool to room temperature before refrigerating. (The sauce will keep for 1 week, covered, in the refrigerator. Reheat gently.)

index

i

table of equivalents

The exact equivalents in the following tables have been rounded for convenience.

LIQUID AND DRY MEASURES

U.S.	METRIC
¼ teaspoon	1.25 milliliters
½ teaspoon	2.5 milliliters
1 teaspoon	5 milliliters
1 tablespoon (3 teaspoons)	15 milliliters
1 fluid ounce (2 tablespoons)	30 milliliters
¼ cup	60 milliliters
⅓ cup	80 milliliters
1 cup	240 milliliters
1 pint (2 cups)	480 milliliters
1 quart (4 cups, 32 ounces)	960 milliliters
1 gallon (4 quarts)	3.84 liters
1 ounce (by weight)	28 grams
1 pound	454 grams
2.2 pounds	1 kilogram

LENGTH MEASURES

U.S.	METRIC
⅛ inch	3 millimeters
¼ inch	6 millimeters
½ inch	12 millimeters
1 inch	2.5 centimeters

OVEN TEMPERATURES

FAHRENHEIT	CELSIUS	GAS
250	120	½
275	140	1
300	150	2
325	160	3
350	180	4
375	190	5
400	200	6
425	220	7
450	230	8
475	240	9
500	260	10